Land Standing

Brian Gay

Copyright © April 2009

Printed in the United States of America

Forward

Advertising sales & management is one of the toughest and the most rewarding jobs someone can choose as a career. Providing marketing solutions and success for diverse businesses in your local community truly allows a successful sale representative to build a career they can be proud of.

Brian Gay's accomplishments in the free paper industry are truly unparalleled. For years industry leaders have relied on Brian's knowledge and leadership. Brian's insight and guidance have been featured in numerous magazines and industry trade journals. This book combines much of Brian's knowledge into one resource to motivate and educate both the new hire and the seasoned professional.

Implementing Brian's strategies contained in this book will allow you to access years of proven strategies to ensure success for you, your advertisers, and your community.

Tim Bingaman
President/CEO
Circulation Verification Council

Table of Contents

001 Introduction
002 15 Minutes at a Time
006 About Geese and a Successful Sales Team
009 Advertising 101?
013 After the Sale
016 Become a Sales Champion
019 Become a Super Star Sales Person
022 Challenge the Experts
025 Change is your Choice
028 Dedication Pays Huge Rewards
031 Do They Know?
034 Elephant Hunting
038 Ending a Sales Slump
041 Evaluate your Way to Success
044 Every Customer is Important
047 Failure is an Event
050 Feeling Professional
053 Get Organized
056 Hints from the Pros
059 How Well do you Know your Paper?
062 I was Once "THE KING"!
065 In Need of Training
068 Is a Computer the Answer?
071 It Costs More Not to Attend!
074 It is a Numbers Game
077 It is not Luck
080 It is Planning Season
084 Just a Reminder

087	"No" Is Almost as Good as "Yes"
090	Not an Objection!
093	Now is the Time
096	Once is not Enough—How Often Should you Advertise?
099	Practice Makes Money
103	Prejudge and Lose
107	Prospecting—The Lifeblood of Sales
110	Saving the Store
113	Selling Success
117	Short Course about Radio
121	So What?
124	Taking a Hard Look
127	The Success Secret
129	The Top Ten (plus 5) Reasons Print Advertising Sales People Fail
133	There Is No "I" in TEAM
136	Truly Amazing
140	Use a Big Eraser
143	We Promise
146	What Advertising Can Do
150	What Happened
153	What have We Lost?
156	What is the Objective?
159	What Successful Sales People Do
162	What We Learned

Introduction

In the summer of 2008 at the age of 62 my dream of tandem skydiving came to pass. I remember being at 10,000 feet saying to myself, "What are you doing? Are you out of your mind?"

As those thoughts raced through my brain, we rolled out of the plane and did 2 complete summersaults and free fell to 3,000 feet reaching a speed of close to 120 miles an hour. The ripcord was pulled and the force slowing us down was about 2 G's. The rest of the decent was like floating in the sky. I was able to control the parachute by pulling on the control lines. As we neared the ground the instructor said that we were going to "Land Standing."

As I thought of a title for this book, "Land Standing" seemed extremely appropriate. In our everyday sales efforts we all strive to "Land Standing." It is in our nature to reach for only our best. My goal in publishing this book is to help everyone selling print advertising to "Land Standing."

I would like to dedicate this book to my wife, Sandy; she has been an inspiration to me for 30 plus years. Sandy is my soul mate and is always there for me.

"The bad news is time flies. The good news is you're the pilot."
—Michael Altshuler

15 Minutes at a Time

Most ad sales jobs are structured so a person can be successful if he or she does the work. The problem is that many think that showing up and being away from home for 8 hours is fulfilling the job requirements. The success comes from working those 8 hours.

Several years ago all 5 of my sales people were complaining that they did not have enough time in the day to get everything accomplished. They said that they had tried arriving early and staying late and nothing helped. They still could not get the job done. The logical conclusion was that we needed another sales person.

I asked them 2 simple questions. "Would you like to make more money?" and "How is your time used each day?" They all said "yes" to more money and started to give some vague answers how they spent their day. No one person could say for sure where all the time went. They were given this challenge. "If you would do one thing for the next 2 weeks that would help you become a really successful sales person and earn more money would you do it?" They all said "yes."

The next morning we had a special 10-minute sales meeting. Each sales person was given 10 sheets of paper—pre-dated for the next 10 days. Eight and a half hours were broken down into 15-minute increments with a small space to write in. For the next 10 working days they would write down what they did the previous 15 minutes. They had to be honest and there would be no reprisal for what was written down. At the end of 2 weeks the sheets would be turned in for me to evaluate. There were some moans and groans about more paper work, but they all decided to do the project.

There was not much talk about the project the first couple of days. By the third day comments came in to my attention. They were surprised how fast 15 minutes went by because they were just talking about what happened last night. They found out how long it took to drive to a customer and make a call. By the fourth day they started to see how much time it took to re do the instructions turned into the composing department. They could see that half an hour lunch was sometimes more like 45 minutes to an hour.

After the end of the fifth day they came to me saying that I had proved my point and that they wanted to stop wasting time writing down what they were doing every 15 minutes. They were reminded of their original agreement and that there was still a week left.

After the 2-week period they all turned in their sheets and the Wednesday sales meeting would be the results of what they had learned and what they had written down. Wednesday morning the sales meeting was rather exciting. The first question asked for each sales person was to tell the others what was one of their major wasting activities. "I always stop for coffee each morning. I thought it was only 10 minutes but it was more like 30." "I always planned for my day each morning. I found that it took me along time to finally leave the office. At least 30 to 45 minutes each day were lost." "I made several trips a day back to the office to drop off ads. If I did that one thing only once during the day I would save almost an hour."

Other comments were just as amazing. "I always do personal errands like dropping off and picking up my dry cleaning as I am out working." "I found that I was making a lot of trips to see customers when they were not in and I would have to go back and make a second call. I could save several hours a week by calling first." "I would stop and see customers who had a limited budget but were nice people because I liked calling on them. They were my friends but they did not buy much advertising."

We then discussed things like, where were you between 8:30 am and 3:30 pm? This is prime selling time. Were you in front of a customer? We talked about territory management. Did you waste a lot of time driving all over your territory and not stopping to see customer in a logical order?

After about 2 weeks the sales started to increase. The sales people were not complaining about too much to do. The Wednesday morning sales meeting was changed to a Wednesday noon meeting (bring your own lunch). It started at noon and was done by 12:30 pm. Time was now viewed as a valuable asset. Everyone started to respect just how important it could be to his or her own success. If they wasted time they wasted opportunity.

We did not hire an additional sales person. The existing sales people all earned more. Were they really successful?

Yes they were. There was very little turnover in the sales staff. We even had a list of other media sales people who wanted to work for us. This one exercise made it possible for the sales people to be the highest-paid advertising sales people in the community.

Action Steps:

- Make a sheet of paper with 15-minute increments. Copy it 9 times.
- Track what you were doing every 15 minutes
- Evaluate the results
- Select 3 or 4 things that were your biggest time wasters
- Take corrective action
- Enjoy your new success

> "Working together works."
> —Dr. Rob Gilbert

About Geese and a Successful Sales Team

When you see geese heading south for the winter flying in a "V" formation, you might be interested in knowing what scientists have discovered about why they fly that way. It has been learned that: As each bird flaps its wings it creates uplift for the bird immediately following. By flying in a "V" formation, the whole flock adds at least 71% more flying range than if each bird flew on its own.

Basic Truth # 1:
A successful sales team shares a common direction and a sense of community and can get where they are going quicker and easier because they are traveling on the thrust of one another.

Whenever a goose falls out of formation, it suddenly feels the drag and the resistance of trying to go alone and quickly gets back into formation to take advantage of the lifting power of the bird immediately in front.

Basic Truth # 2:
A successful sales team member gains strength, power, and safety in numbers when traveling in the same direction as others with whom they share a common goal.

When the lead goose gets tired, he or she rotates back in the formation and another goose flies to the point.

Basic Truth # 3:
Successful sales team members take turns leading the way. It is not always intentional. It happens because of the sales cycle and because something or someone has inspired a sales person.

The geese honk from behind to encourage those up front to keep up their speed.

Basic Truth # 4:
A successful sales team knows we all need to be remembered with active support and praise. A sincere positive attitude is part of every successful sales team.

Finally, when a goose gets sick or is wounded and falls out, 2 geese fall out of formation and follow him or her down to help and protect. They stay with the downed goose until the crisis resolves and then they launch out on their own or with another formation to catch up with their group.

Basic Truth # 5:
A successful sales team stands by each other in times of need and they are willing to lend a helping hand or give needed direction. If one member lands in the hospital it is amazing how quick the rest of the team is willing to step up and cover the accounts.

We are fortunate that there are more geese in successful sales teams than turkeys. When you work outside of the team you miss the uplifting effect of all the other members of the sales team. By working together you will enjoy at least 71% more range. Let us remember to uphold each other in friendship and in prayer each day—and to give each other a big "honk" now and then!

Action Steps:
- Develop a TEAM attitude
- Work toward your common goal
- Give credit to others
- Enjoy being a team player

(*The basic wording was sent to me by e-mail. I do not know the identity of the original author. I took the liberty to adapt it to fit this article.*)

"The most important thing about a quote is to hear what it says."

Advertising 101?

Every so often, I feel that my education is just not complete. I took a course in advertising while in college, but must admit I do not remember much at all. The thought of pulling out a college textbook on advertising principles is about as exciting as watching corn grow. (You laugh. Couple of years ago the most popular web site from Iowa set up a webcam to show a corn field. Thousands of people would go to this site each day to see the corn grow.) The more I thought about my lack of education about advertising the more it bothered me. My claim to fame in college is that I help make the top half of my class possible. When I looked back, what was remembered from my college courses were a few quotes and where to go to find information. That is when I decided to skip the textbook and go directly to the quotes. After all, you will get an entire year of Principles of Advertising without reading the textbook, (remember Cliff Notes?) but in the end you will know the quotes everyone should have remembered.

With a little help from the AAF e-newsletter here goes.

> "Be civil to all; sociable to many, familiar with few, friend to one; enemy to none."
> —Benjamin Franklin, member, *Advertising Hall of Fame*

This was remembered because it seemed to fit all situations. As a person involved in sales this applies to your daily life.

> "I have always believed that writing advertisements is the second most profitable form of writing. The first, of course, is ransom notes."
> —Philip Dusenberry, member, *Advertising Hall of Fame*

If you do not think this is true hire an agency to write a paragraph or two. Think about it, a well-written advertisement is the key to the success of a business and is of great value.

> "Advertising makes people discontented. It makes them want things they don't have. Without discontent, there is no progress, no achievement."
> —Morris Hite, member, *Advertising Hall of Fame*

What an ad does is create the desire in the consumer to take action and buy the product. Nothing will happen until that desire is created. The desire to own a product leads to the discontent.

> "You can say the right thing about a product and nobody will listen. You've got to say it in such a way that people will feel it in their gut. Because if they don't feel it, nothing will happen."
> —William Bernbach, member, *Advertising Hall of Fame*

Often the buying process is an emotional decision. People want to know that they are making the right choice.

If you provide them with that feeling they will feel it and respond.

> "Creativity is a highfalutin word for the work I have to do between now and Tuesday."
> —Ray Kroc, member, *Advertising Hall of Fame*

This is one of those truisms of advertising. Nothing happens until you do the work.

> "Luck is a dividend of sweat. The more you sweat, the luckier you get."
> —Ray Kroc, member, *Advertising Hall of Fame*

In the final analysis in order to make advertising work you must be willing to do the job correctly and put in the time required to make your customers succeed.

> "In good times, people want to advertise; in bad times, they have to."
> —Bruce Barton, member, *Advertising Hall of Fame*

You have to help your advertisers and become a player in their success. It is easier to convince people to advertise when they are not worried about money. A real sales person makes sure they advertise when times are not so good.

> "There is no better test of an advertisement than whether or not it actually sells the product! In fact, it is the only true way of determining if your advertisement works."
> —John Caples, member, *Advertising Hall of Fame*

Results are what customers want from advertising. Be sure to ask how an ad worked and always suggest ways to improve your customers' advertising. How well it works is really a test of you and your paper.

"If each of us hires people who are smaller than we are, we shall become a company of dwarfs. But if each of us hires people who are bigger than we are, we shall become a company of giants."
—David Ogilvy, member, *Advertising Hall of Fame*

This was thrown in because it is true and it may also be the beginning of my next college course—Human Resource 101?

Action Steps:
- Start keeping track of quotes that are important to you
- Search for a familiar thread in the quotes you have collected
- This thread will help define who you really are
- Work to improve your life

"The price of greatness is responsibility."
—Winston Churchill

After the Sale

One of the hardest aspects of selling is to learn what should happen after the sale. So much emphasis is placed on the sale itself that the sales person assumes that his or her job is finished. After all, in one way or another their compensation is based on the fact that they make sales. It is easy to lose sight that the sale does not end with the order. The sales person is the responsible party, as far as the customer is concerned, until the ad is printed and distributed in an acceptable manner.

Good customer relationships begin with timely follow-up on requests and commitments. If your customer wants a new rate card, tear sheets, or copy of your paper with the ad that you sold in it, you as the sales person are responsible to make sure those requests are honored. While you can delegate the task to someone else, the responsibility falls on you as the sales person.

Complaints and unhappy customers are a part of the job. A successful sales person learns how to handle the situation. Customers are not upset with you. They are upset with the situation. They are smart enough to know that you did not intentionally cause the problem. They are frustrated and you as the sales person are their contact person. You sold them the ad and they feel you will help them. A true sales person never takes this situation as a personal complaint. It is not about the sales person, it is about the event.

Successful sales people solve account problems. Whenever there is a mistake in the ad they call their customers as soon as they find out. Do not make the mistake of thinking that the customer will not notice an error. They will. If the price for a gallon of milk was printed as $0.99 instead of $1.99 call customers and tell them. Do not wait until customers demand milk for half price. There are things you can do and often it is as simple as writing a letter explaining that your publication made a mistake on the pricing. Then make enough copies so every check out line has one. Tape them to the door and on the milk case. Own up to the mistake. If you wait to call, it will only make matters worse. If the customer calls you it is a lot worse!

When a customer calls and is irate, the best thing a sales person can do is listen to the customer and understand that he or she wants to vent frustration on some one. When this happens you listen. You do not interrupt. You do not argue. You do not contradict. Let the customer say what he or she wants to say. If the customer is wrong then discuss the issue calmly and explain yourself. If you or your paper is at fault admit it and discuss amends. If your manager does not allow you to give credits or wants to discuss these types of situations with you before you offer something to the customer, then tell the customer that you are going to your manager and explain what happened and ask him or her for corrective action. In this situation you have just become an ally with your customer. That is what the customer wanted when he or she called. The responsibility of making the customer satisfied now rests with the manager. Often times, if you ask the customer what he or she feels is fair the suggestion for corrective action is a lot less than what you have in mind. This is also useful information to pass on to your manager. After you talk to your manager, call the customer and explain the outcome of the discussion and make sure everyone is in agreement.

Just remember this simple quote from Martin Luther King Jr. "The time is always right to do what is right." This truly applies to dealing with your customers before and after the sale is made.

Action Steps:

- Practice following up on your commitments
- When a mistake happens, call the customer immediately
- Always do the right thing

> *"You cannot control what happens to you, but you can control your attitude toward what happens to you, and in that, you will be mastering change rather than allowing it to master you."*
> —Brian Tracy

Become a Sales Champion

When Olympic athletes are going to run the 100-yard dash, they do not just walk up to the starting blocks, get set, and run the race. They are trained and conditioned for this moment. They have visualized winning the race thousands of times. They have run the race in their mind over and over again. The visualization makes them champions.

Just like an Olympic athlete you have trained to sell ads for your paper. You know the ins and outs of your publication and competing media. You continue to get training about selling print advertising. So to speak, you have trained and conditioned yourself to make sales presentations. Do you use the internal power of visualization to increase sales? If not, you should. This simple technique can give you big rewards. To become a sale champion try this uncomplicated exercise for the next month. Just before you go in to make a sales call, visualize yourself making that call. What are your first words? How do you greet the customer? Are you smiling? Do you act interested in the customer? Can you see yourself asking for the order? Do you see yourself making the sale?

This is a lot more than just wishing for success. It is a way to get you in the mindset of a winner and a successful sales person. It takes about 15 to 20 seconds to visualize a typical sales call. Try it and you will find that you are working up to your potential. You will also increase sales. Your customers will start to treat you as a success because you give the impression that you are a success. You come across as someone who is knowledgeable and comfortable with what you are selling and surveys prove that people like to buy from that type of sales person.

Your sales presentations will go much smoother since you have visualized yourself giving it numerous times. It is becoming a natural way for you to sell. Because you are visualizing before you make the call, you will also be aware what is happening during the call. You are no longer wondering what to say next. You are in charge of the sales presentation. Visualizing helps you after the call because you can adapt. This is important since you can make changes that need to be made before the next call.

If you believe that most people want to buy from a sales person who is polite, friendly, knowledgeable, prepared, self assured, and successful, then add visualizing to your sales preparation. Try it for 30 days and you will see why it is powerful.

Action Steps:

- Start taking a few seconds before each call and practice visualization
- Learn to see yourself making the call
- Always visualize that you closed the sale and got the order
- Your attitude about yourself will improve and you are viewed as a successful sales person

> "The difference between a successful person and others is not a lack of strength, not a lack of knowledge, but rather a lack of will."
> —Vince Lombardi

Become a Super Star Sales Person

Have you ever wished that you could think fast on your feet? Are you good at giving presentations to major accounts? Do you feel relaxed when speaking in front of customers? Do you represent your publication in a professional manner? If you answered "yes" to all of these questions, then a great deal of time has been spent training and educating you as a sales person.

Most of you had to answer "no" to one or all of the questions. In order to answer "yes" to all of the above questions someone has to set up the necessary training and schedule the sessions. At a small publication, it is difficult, if not impossible, to have someone on staff to handle training needs. There is just not money in the budget for such a person. Consequently, training is allowed to take a back seat, not because the value is not recognized, but it requires so much from an already stretched manager or publisher.

There is a way to get all of this training for a cost of about $60.00 a year for weekly training. That figures out to just over $1.00 a week. The necessary training is available at your local Toastmasters Club. Most of these clubs meet for an hour each week and have a structured meeting planned, conducted, and presented by the individual members. It is an organization that trains people how to speak and communicate effectively. They train people how to prepare, how to be leaders, how to be confident, and how to be professional.

Many people have the same preconceived idea about Toastmasters as I had a few years ago. I thought that the only people who would join such an organization had to be a little weird or loved to hear themselves talk. Giving a presentation in front of a crowd never really bothered me. But, if I had joined Toastmasters early in my career as a sales person, I would have been a super star. My ranking would have been in the top 10% instead of the top 25%. The difference in terms of actual dollars in the pocket would have been in the tens of thousands.

If I were a sales manager or a publisher today, one of the requirements for all of the sales people would be to attend and complete the first Toastmasters manual. It would take 6 months to a year and the company would invest in the fee. All new sales people would be told that this is part of their training and is a requirement. There is no better a value than the training people receive by participating in Toastmasters. If you have doubts, visit a few meetings yourself, it costs nothing to visit. You will witness these positive changes in people right before your eyes. They become confident, professional, relaxed, assured, and are willing to participate and lead. (Those are the attributes of a super star sales person.)

What are you waiting for? Is your sales career worth an investment of $60.00? Will you be nervous when you give your first speech at a Toastmasters Meeting? The answer is "yes". Will you overcome that fear? Again the answer is "yes". But, if you do not try something new to improve yourself you will always be what you are now. For information about Toastmasters visit their web site at **www.toastmasters.org.** This web site contains all the information you need to find a club and learn about Toastmasters. Toastmasters is a sure-fire recipe on how to become a super star sales person.

Action Steps:

- Check out the Toastmasters web site
- Find a club near you and visit it
- Invest in your success
- Make the commitment to change

"The way to get started is to quit talking and begin doing."
—Walt Disney

Challenge the Experts

Up until May 6, 1954, so called experts from all over the world declared no human could run a mile in less than 4 minutes. They had all sorts of studies that pompously proclaimed that no runner could break the 4-minute mile. Presumably, a human could not run that far, that fast, for that length of time. For years, these experts were right. No one ever ran a mile in less than 4 minutes.

However, on that fateful day a young 25-year-old British medical student did not take the opinions of the experts to heart and ran a mile in 3 minutes 59.4 seconds. Roger Bannister became the first man to run a mile in less than 4 minutes.

What is more amazing is in the next 10 years 336 other runners ran a mile in less than 4 minutes. The obstacle to running a 4-minute mile was all in the runners' minds. For years, the athletes believed the experts and were convinced that it was an impossibility to accomplish such an amazing feat.

As a sales person, how often has someone told you that a certain business will not advertise in your paper? Just like the experts' theory that no human could break the 4-minute mile, it is now a truism that the business will not advertise in your paper. Everyone believes that the business will not advertise, so no one bothers to make a call. How many of these businesses are in your territory? How many do you drive past every day and never stop because you heard that they would not advertise in your paper?

Because you believe what you are told by the older sales people, you are perpetuating the belief. As long as you believe what they say, that the business will not advertise, it will not. Unless you break out of this mindset, the belief continues to be true. Year after year, you are proving that the business will never advertise in your paper. The main reason that this happens is that as a sales person you keep driving by the business day in, day out, and never stop to give them the opportunity to place an ad. You are contributing to the myth.

Why not take action and figure out just how many "never will advertise in your paper" businesses are in your territory. Then compile a list and form a plan on how you are going to contact each one of them. Maybe the first call is an introductory call. Maybe the second call is to find out a little more about the business and the people who own or operate the business. This is all plus business. When any one of these non-advertising businesses invests in an ad, you have gained additional business. Remember that account was one that would never advertise in your paper. It is an account that your paper never had.

Sales people complain all the time that there is not enough new business moving into their territory to increase their sales. A true sales professional realizes that there is a huge opportunity in the businesses that do not advertise. As a professional it is your job, no it is your duty, to change the cycle and work with these potential advertisers.

Many years ago, a large American shoe manufacture sent 2 sales reps out to different parts of the Australian outback to see if they could drum up some business among the Aborigines. Some time later, the company received telegrams from both sales people.

The first one said, "No business here. Natives don't wear shoes."

The second one said, "Great opportunity here. Natives don't wear shoes!"

It all depends on how you view your territory. I would suspect that it is a "Great opportunity—many more business need to advertise in our paper."

Action Steps:
- Make a commitment to contact the non-advertisers in your territory
- Develop a plan
- Follow your plan
- Reap the benefit from this new opportunity

"When you are through changing, you are through."
—Bruce Barton, member, Advertising Hall of Fame

Change is your Choice

Have you ever thought back to the times that you have been most successful in your career? Do you recall the feeling you had? Were you nervous? Were you a little unsure? These are all natural feelings that a person has when he or she decides to break away and try something different. Many of us get trapped in the same old rut. We go to work, call on the customers, make some sales, earn a decent living, and soon believe that that is all there is to life.

I am suggesting it is time to shake things up a bit. Maybe, to start, you drive to work using a different route. Maybe you could start making one more cold call a day. How about setting your goal for the year to earn just $2000.00 more? Whatever you decide to do you will be making a change. You will be experiencing something out of your comfort zone. The thrill and an excitement of doing something new makes your entire day go better.

Getting stuck in the same routine is living a slow death. The enthusiasm in life happens because of change. Change is the catalyst that makes life rewarding. As many of you are aware, I made a major change in my life. I decided to become healthy and lose weight. My decision was to have bariatric bypass surgery. The decision was based on several factors. I was extremely over weight. I was close to developing several health issues. I had tried on my own to lose weight but was never able to make it last. I was a yo-yo dieter. I would drop 10 pounds and gain back 15. That was how my life went. I lost the enthusiasm for life and needed a drastic change.

The second reason I chose this route was the need for a proven plan that would work. The program was clearly defined and if I were to accept the plan, the surgery, and do exactly what I was told to do I would be successful. I had a team of 4 people all helping me succeed. Does this start to sound familiar? You have a manager to help you succeed. You have an association that brings in dynamic speakers to help you succeed. You have access to numerous books, tapes, DVDs, and seminars to help you with your new goal and your success. Your part in all of this is to make the decision to change.

Once you do decide to improve your life by making a change, your entire attitude about yourself and those around you improves. You will find yourself seeking new adventures and thriving on the change in your life. You will no longer be fearful of change but rather enjoy the rush that comes whenever you try something new. You will want to do many of the things you have put off doing for one reason or the other.

Two years ago I would never have dreamed that I would skydive. But, I did. It was a tandem jump from almost 2 miles up. We free fell for the first 7,000 feet, deployed the chute, and glided to a perfect landing. I am not suggesting that you do the same thing. I am suggesting that you break away from your routine and start enjoying life. After all, the choice to change is yours. I am so glad I made that choice.

Action Steps:
- Make a commitment to change some aspect of your life
- Seek outside expertise to ensure your success
- Follow a proven plan
- Enjoy the change and your new life

> "It is one of the most beautiful compensations in life . . . we can never help another without helping ourselves."
> —Ralph Waldo Emerson

Dedication Pays Huge Rewards

Several years ago I cut a small article from *Success*. It was written by Harvey Mackay and titled "Dedication Pays."

A business acquaintance describes the brilliant marketing practices of Billy Graham:

> "He is the best salesman I ever met. He sells salvation—a product no one has ever seen, heard, smelled, touched, or tasted. If his techniques were graded by traditional standards, he would probably snare a C+. He is not a particularly glib speaker, nor is he noted for his jokes. He would not claim to be a great Bible scholar, and he has thousands of competitors. Yet he is the best in the world at what he does.
>
> Why? Because of his dedication to his "customers." Every action he takes is designed to meet their needs, not his own. And it shows."

As a print advertising sales person do you show how dedicated you are to your customers, or are you trying to make a few dollars more in commission? Many sales people are only looking out for themselves. They worry that they are not selling enough, preoccupied about their competitors, or thinking about what is in it for them. Diane Ciotta, a well-known sales trainer for print advertising sales people, sums it up by saying, "Your customers do not care how much you know until they know how much you care."

Every successful sales person will tell you the same thing in one form or another. The key to success in selling is taking care of the customer. Your mind has to accept that your job is taking care of your customers. You will earn more and achieve your goals when you worry more about them and less about yourself.

You need to prepare for each call and not just "wing it" as so many sales people do. Caring for your customer is to make sure you are not wasting their time. As a print advertising sales person it is your job to come up with new ideas, suggestions, ad campaigns, and be able to explain why you feel your suggestions will help their business. You need to ask questions about their business so you can help them. They want you to be the expert. However, they first want to know that you care about them.

My guess the number one reason an advertiser stops using your paper is because the sales person did not show that he or she cared enough. If the job only required you to go out and pick up ads, anyone could do it. You have to be dedicated to your customers. Every action you take must be designed to meet their needs, not your own. As stated above, you do not have to be the most skilled sales person, or the best at telling jokes. You do have to be the best you can at showing your customers that you are dedicated to them and their business.

This is a winning attitude that will make you a super advertising sales person. Your customer dedication will surely show.

> **Action Steps:**
> - Be committed to serving your customers first
> - Prepare for each sales call as if it was your most important call because it is
> - Be willing to do the little extras that show you care
> - Remember—We can never help another without helping ourselves

"It's the little things that make the big things possible. Only close attention to the fine details of any operation makes the operation first class."
—J. Willard Marriott

Do They Know?

Have you ever worked with an account for quite sometime only to find out that they bought a product or a service you could supply from some one else? You go over everything you did or said to see why you did not get the order. After agonizing over a missed sale, you still do not have a clue. Do you just mark it up as a lost sale? Do you just move forward realizing that you cannot make every sale? While that is true, what is also true is that the number one reason people do not buy from you is that they do not know what you sell.

Recently, while working on a national committee, we were charged with finding a company to do some sophisticated database development work for us. We sent out requests for bids to everyone we could think of as well as asked others if they knew of a company that did the kind of work we were interested in. We were successful in finding a company that had done similar work for other companies and understood our needs. We contracted with them and the project was started. It was not until the final stages of the project did one of our regular suppliers ask why they were not offered a chance to bid. Even though we had worked with this supplier for several years on an on going basis, not one committee member was aware that this supplier could provide the service we needed. Consequently, the very people we had a strong working relationship with did not even get a chance at the sale.

Does this happen with your customers? Do they believe that all you sell is space in your paper? Do they know that you can distribute inserts? Do they know that the inserts can be delivered to specific zip codes and/or zones? Does your paper offer a print and deliver program and if it does do your customers know? Do your customers know that you can help them do complete promotions for their store or business? Do your customers know that you can help them prepare an advertising budget? Do your customers know that your paper is audited and that along with the audit, readership studies are done that may help them plan for future business?

Years ago one of my sale reps made a mistake and scheduled a customer's inserts a week too early. We did not find out about the mistake until the papers were on the street being delivered. The only thing to be done was to go to the customer and tell him. Lucky for us the sale items were already at the store. We offered to help stock the shelves. The customer declined the offer. I then proposed to print and deliver a 4-page tab insert filled with products he wanted to sell in his store. We offered to do the composition, printing, and distribution at no cost as a way of making up for our mistake. His comment, "You can do inserts?" We started talking about his needs and what he wanted to do. We were a perfect fit for his needs. We had extra time in the composing department.

The printing would fit into the schedule on one of the slower days. Within 48 hours we were back with a proposal for inserts. Over the next several years we printed inserts 26 times a year for this customer. Often the run was increased to include other papers in surrounding areas. How much business did we lose because our customer did not know we could produce inserts? He saw us as an insert delivery business. No one had ever told him about what we could do.

The above stories point out just how important it is for your customers to understand all that your publication has to offer. It is not the customer's responsibility to find out what your capabilities are. Maybe a quality list for additional new business is your present account list. Be sure to inform them about all of your products and services. If your customers do not know what you sell—how can they buy it from you?

Action Steps:

- Prepare a list of all the products and services your paper offers
- Start a campaign to inform your customers about all you can do
- Talk to your customers about their special needs
- Enjoy the additional sales you will make

"The big secret in life is that there is no big secret. Whatever your goal, you can get there if you're willing to work."

—Oprah Winfrey

Elephant Hunting

Many situations arise during the course of being an advertising sales person. The one that cause the most internal excitement is when a new sales person runs into first major account and is successful at obtaining an appointment to present the paper. The first thought is how much easier my job will be when that account is advertising every week. The second thought is feeling of being just a little smug. For the next few days everything else is put on hold while the sales person prepares for this one important call. There is so much that needs to be in the proposal. Often the sales person believes that he or she has to cover every base and end up with a proposal that weighs a couple of pounds. The day finally arrives. The sales person tells his or her story and leaves the proposal. All during the call the customer seemed to be interested and even agreed with the sales person on several points.

The sales person leaves and goes back to the office confident that the advertising will start arriving any day. After a month or so the sales person has not heard a word. He or she calls the customer and is told that the person is not available and the sales person leaves a voice message. After all the sales process is still going forward because they did not say "no". After waiting for a few more weeks, another call is placed with the same results. After a while the sales person stops calling.

Many of us call this sales approach "elephant hunting." While bringing down an elephant supplies food for a long time, the sales person needs to hunt smaller game to be able to survive until the elephant is dropped. The excitement of landing that one huge account has caused many sales people to die along the way.

First of all, in order to hunt elephants the hunter must spend an enormous amount of time learning about elephants. The sales person needs to know everything possible about that major account. The hunter will read books, magazines, and articles about hunting elephants. The sales person will read books, trade journals, and articles about the major account and the industry. The hunter will research the proper location, equipment, and skill needed to hunt the elephant. Likewise, the sales person will research the needs of the customer and gain an understanding of the needs of the account. Only when the hunter is confident that they have the knowledge will they schedule a hunt. The sales person will still be unclear about certain aspects of the major account's business and will start fact finding.

The hunter is now serious about hunting the elephant and the sales person is serious about pursuing the major account. While the hunter asks questions of other hunters the sales person asks for a meeting with the potential major account. Both have the same goal of acquiring more information. The hunter knows that other hunters love to talk about their exploits. The sales person also knows the major account likes to talk about the company. They both ask questions and learn. The hunter wants to know how others have been successful. The sales person wants to know how they advertise now and if there are areas where the present advertising is not working. The sales person also wants to know if he or she makes a recommendation to improve return on advertising investment can that person make a decision. The sales person must also be willing to listen and take in everything.

The hunter has decided where to go to hunt the elephant and everything is arranged. It is hard to believe that he has already spent a year just to get this far. Likewise the sales person is ready to proceed. It has only been 9 months and a great deal of hours after work to get to the presentation stage. All this time, both the hunter and the sales rep have been preparing for this event. Will they be successful? The elephants may never show up. The major account may decide to not make a change.

How many employers will allow a sales person 9 months to make a presentation? How did the sales person survive for 9 months? The answer is he or she never allowed the allure of a major account to consume the working life. The sales person knew that he or she had to make sales on a consistent basis in order to keep his job. The major account did not just fall into the sales person's lap. It was cultivated for 9 months.

Action Steps:

- Commit to working 100% on your regular business then work on a major account
  (This is something you do in addition to your regular selling)
- Research a major account before you ever make a presentation
- When you meet the major account for the first time, do a needs analysis
- Be patient and persistent
- Be prepared for a long sales cycle

> *"In any moment of decision, the best thing you can do is the right thing: the next best thing is the wrong thing: and the worst thing you can do is nothing."*
> —Theodore Roosevelt

Ending a Sales Slump

I often get writer's block. It is that terrible feeling knowing a deadline is near and there is not an original idea or thought worth writing about. It is better described as writer's slump. Tell a few friends and they are all sympathetic about the problem. The best way for me to overcome the slump is to start writing. Once the writing starts then there is a resurgence of ideas and creativity. It often takes several tries before anything worthwhile is written. The act of starting to write lifts the writer's block for me.

Sales people often have a sales slump. When they tell their friends there is not much sympathy shown. People somehow expect sales people to always be in a selling mode. They tend to believe that the sales person is just not working very hard at their job rather than being in a slump. That it is all a numbers game and if enough calls are made then the results are assured. Nothing could be further from the truth. Once a sales person is in a slump things will get worst unless there is a way to turn it around.

What will turn it around for you? It is hard to say, however here are some ideas that may help:

1. Ask a successful sales person in your office if you can ride with them for a day. After each call ask questions about what you just witnessed. This day will provide you with some insight in what is working with a successful sales person. You will also learn that the two of you have more in common in your sales effort than you once thought.
2. Attend a sales session at a paper association meeting. Spend a Saturday learning how to be a better sales person. The real benefit is that you will see all level of sales people learning how to do their job better. Many of them would have been where you are—in a slump.
3. Schedule 5 solid sales calls and go to them prepared. Go back to the way you sold when you first started. Remember being so prepared for a call it was scary. Try it again and you might find what you are doing wrong.
4. After each call do a personal evaluation. Take out a legal pad and write down everything that just happened in the call. At the end of the day study these pages and see if there is a common theme to them. Look at what went well and what went wrong.
5. Ask someone to ride with you to observe your sales technique. This is a great way to spend time with your sales manager. Sales managers are a great resource for information because they have been where you are and have become successful.
6. Nothing beats practice. Practice your sales call before you see the customer. Practice in front of a

mirror or ask a friend to critique your presentation. Practice does make perfect.
7. Use the power of visualization. This is an extremely powerful way to get out of a slump. If you visualize yourself making the presentation, just before giving it, you will be surprised how well the actual presentation goes. You have in affect set your mind into the selling mode and took that with you on the sales call.
8. Think positively. Nothing can make you feel better about yourself than to have a positive attitude. By erasing the doubts you leave your brain open to succeed.

The sales slump is one of the most agonizing things that can happen to a sales person. The sooner you get back on track the better you will feel and the better you will do your job. The key is to take action to end the sales slump as soon as possible. Every sales person experiences a sales slump and the successful ones have ways to overcome it and carry on.

Action Steps:
- Take action as soon as you feel yourself going into a slump
- Select one of the ideas above and use it
- Think Positive thoughts about yourself
- Keep moving forward
- Do not stop working

> "A clear vision, backed by definite plans, gives you a tremendous feeling of confidence and personal power."
>
> —Brian Tracy, Author

Evaluate your Way to Success

Do you keep track of your sales activity? Do you know how many cold calls you made last week? How many proposals did you present? How much time was spent taking care of customer issues? How many times did you ask for the order last week? If you are like most sales people, you could not answer all of the above questions. That seems strange when you stop and think about it. By answering these questions, you are allowing your sales effort to be evaluated. Your sales manager cannot help you until you have answers to questions that explain your sales activity.

Making cold calls is not everyone's most exciting thing to do. Consequently, it is easy to avoid making them. There is always something else to do. You can go to your computer and start working on redefining the readership study to fit the client. You can spend extra time reviewing your cold call list. Maybe you could spend time just building your cold call list. The result is not making the cold calls. These cold calls need to be done in a systematic way. There has to be time set aside to cold call. You may be able to do calls by telephone. If you are an outside advertising sales rep, most likely, you will have to do a combination of using the telephone and making the cold calls in person.

How many cold calls should you make each week depends on how long you have been in the job. A new sales person needs to set making cold calls as their top priority. After building a client base, and when advertisers are placing orders with you regularly, you can cut back on the total number of cold calls. Nevertheless, you can never stop completely. You need a constant flow of new customers to replace those that you have lost for one reason or another. Be sure to write down in your appointment calendar just how many cold calls you made each day.

It is easy to keep track of proposals that you have presented, or spec ads that you suggested to the client. All you have to do is write the total number each day in your appointment calendar. If you are only doing these activities a few times a month, you need to pick up the effort. Proposals and spec ads work. Sales people who get into that habit sell more print ads than most.

We all think that when we make a sales presentation we are asking for the order. That is not true. Do not get into the trap where you honestly believe that you are so good at presenting that the client will jump up and say they want to buy the ad. After every sales call you need to ask yourself, "Did I ask them to buy the ad?" Be honest and you will be surprised how many times you did not ask for the sale. Asking for the sale has to be such that both parties know that you are asking for the order.

Now is the hard part. If the customer said "no" did you try to find out what the customer's objection really was? Did you restate the objection then overcome it and ask for the order the second time. Most sales people do not ask for the order a second time. Record how many times a day you asked for the order in your appointment book. Give yourself a star for each time you asked for the order a second time.

The point of all of this is to get you to start recording sales activity. How many thank you cards did you send out last week? How much time did you spend taking care of customer problems? How much time did you spend in the office planning your week and day? Once you have answers to these questions you will be able to help yourself and your sales manager get you back on track if you are in a slump. You will be able to judge what is driving your sales success. There is no one that can evaluate your sales activity if you do not have an understanding of the activities that you are doing on a regular basis. You are the key to your success. Evaluating your activity is the best way to know if you are staying the course.

Action Steps:

- Commit to tracking your activity
- Make a sheet that lists all sales activity such as cold calls, account service calls, proposals, number of times you asked for the order, proposal given, spec ads presented, and so on
- Make a copy of the list for each day
- Check off what you actually did after each call
- After a couple of weeks, set up appointment with your manager to review your activity
- Make necessary adjustments to ensure your success

> *"There is only one boss. The customer. And he can fire everybody in the company from the chairman on down, simply by spending his money somewhere else."*
> —Sam Walton

Every Customer is Important

Everyone is talking about regional and national accounts. Publishers, GMs, and sales people see this segment as the way to succeed and earn fantastic commissions. We all know of a story where a sales person was in the right place at the right time and landed one huge client that ensured their success forever. In fact, most of us dream about just such an account. It is estimated that the national advertising placed in all newspapers was $7 billion in 2007. On the other hand, the local advertisers placed $35.2 billion. That means, about 17% of all newspaper advertising came from regional and national accounts.

Step back for a moment. What are some of the things we will do for that business? First of all, no one in their right mind would call on one of those huge accounts without preparing a sales presentation. There would be charts and graphs, demographic data, readership studies, rate cards, and a copy of the latest audit. The sales person would be nervous for days trying to learn as much as possible about the national account. After all this is one of the "big boys."

If the national accounts only represent 17% of the business, imagine what advertising sales people do for the other 83% of the business. In fact, most of the time, the local advertiser is treated without any fanfare at all. Most sales people do not bother to prepare for the call. There is no proposal, no presentation, no charts and graphs, no readership studies, no explanation of the circulation audit, and no time researching the advertiser's business. Yet week after week the sales person expects to get ads.

What would happen if the sales person started doing some of the things that they know national media buyers want and need on a local level? What would happen if the sales person started providing the customer with ideas for special promotions? What would happen if the sales person actually went into the store and talked to the owner about how the advertising budget should be spent each month? There are all sorts of statistics that show when the best months for each kind of store to run more advertising. How would the customer react if they receive a thank you note from the sales person?

Think about it. If a customer runs an average of a quarter page a week that customer is buying 13 full pages a year. What would you do to get a national account to run 13 full pages with you over the next year? It is strange; we treat a national advertiser better than our local advertisers. The customer buying a quarter page a week will be charged more than a national advertiser doing a full page a month. We do not reward the loyal week in and week out advertiser but we are sure to reward a national advertiser. Most of the added value in our products is saved for the big hitters.

The lesson in all of this is simple. Treat the local advertisers as if they are the ones that will guarantee your success—because they will. These local customers control 84% of the available funds in your market for newspaper advertising. They want you to step forward and become a partner in growing their business. They want you to give them sound advice about their advertising. They often look to you as the expert. If you treat these local customers with the same respect you would show a national advertiser you can guarantee your own success. Will it be easy? Will you make every sale? The answer to both questions is "no." However, your sales position will become more rewarding. You will become a respected person in the community. You will watch your sales grow year after year.

When that national account does come along you will know exactly how to proceed. After all, you treat all your customers as if they are the most important customers you have.

Action Steps:

- Commit to treating all your customers the same
- Talk to your local accounts to determine their needs
- Invest extra time in yourself and your job
- Be prepared for every call
- Enjoy your success

> *"Failure is not a person but an event."*
> —Zig Zigler

Failure is an Event

Every so often we hear something that is so profound that it changes the way we think and act. A few years ago, I was listening to one of those motivational tapes while driving. The speaker was Zig Zigler and he said, "Failure is not a person but an event."

Think about it. You can fail at an event and you are not a failure. You can fail at a sales call and go to the next because you are not a failure. You may not be a very good cook and ruin a dinner but you are not a failure. The dinner may be a failure, but you are not. Knowing that a person is not a failure allows you to be more open to new ideas. You can be more open to risking a little of yourself and cold calling on that potential customer. If Thomas Edison had considered himself a failure we would not have the electric light. While his quest for the right filament failed hundreds of times he never thought that he was a failure. Each experiment got him that much closer to the solution.

Selling is a lot like Edison's process of inventing the light bulb. Sales people do not always make a sale on every call. But do they see this as something personal or an event. All too often they take the set back as something personal. If there happens to be several such outcomes in a row then the tendency is to view the dealings as a personal failure even more. A sales person who views such a string of negative happenings as a personal failure, instead of a series of events, will develop call reluctance and stop doing what will change things.

This is the track record of another famous American:

- Failed in business at age 22
- Ran for the legislature and was defeated at age 23
- Again failed in business at age 24
- Elected to the legislature at age 25
- Sweetheart died at age 26
- Had a nervous breakdown at age 27
- Defeated for Speaker at age 29
- Defeated for the Senate at age 29
- Defeated for an elector at age 31
- Defeated for Congress at age 34
- Elected to Congress at age 37
- Defeated for Congress at age 39
- Defeated for the Senate at age 46
- Defeated for Vice President at age 47
- Defeated for the Senate at age 49
- Elected as the President of the United States at age 51

Even with all the set backs, Abraham Lincoln is viewed by many as the best President this country has ever had. He must have known that many events in his life may have been failures, but he never viewed himself as a failure. Every day you call on customers and potential customers and offer advertising opportunities. Not all of them buy, but that does not mean you are a failure. Your success as a sales person happens because you try again. What will change the situation is to keep trying. It is time to adopt the attitude that "failure is an event and not a person." Once you do, then trying one more time is a natural way of life. That is all you have to do. When faced with a failure try one more time. Edison did. Lincoln did. You can too.

Action Steps:
- Adopt a "failure is an event attitude"
- Commit to always trying one more time
- Remember your successes
- Enjoy your new attitude

"Know yourself. Don't accept your dog's admiration as conclusive evidence that you are wonderful."
—Ann Landers

Feeling Professional

The other night, I was watching Larry King and his guest was well-known news reporter, who started his radio career while still in high school in 1933. He has a syndicated news show on the radio every day except Sunday. The broadcast is carried on 1200 radio stations and 400 Armed Forces Network radio stations worldwide. There sat this gentleman who is in his 80s and is dressed in a suit and tie and looks immaculate.

Larry King keeps asking his guest questions about his career and all of the amazing events he has reported on in his broadcasts. The stories are intriguing. Larry then asks if it is true that whenever he is behind the microphone and doing his show he wears a coat and a tie. The guest replied "yes" it was true except for a few days early in his career.

It seems using his common sense, he decided that since he was on radio he should dress more casual. After all, no one saw him outside of the other people in the studio. Besides, it is a lot more expensive to wear suits and ties every day. He started showing up for work in business casual attire and broadcasting his radio show. After

3 days he asked the engineer, who worked his show, how he thought the show had gone. The engineer bluntly said that it was not up to normal high standards and that there was something missing.

Larry's guest went home and thought about what he had done differently and the only thing was the way he dressed for work. The more he thought about it the more he realized that he did not give his best unless he looked his best. It did not matter that no one could see him. What mattered is how he felt about himself.

The important part of this story is not that you need to dress like a professional every day. The lesson is that you have to feel good about yourself and feel professional. If wearing a coat and a tie makes you feel professional then you should do just that. At our office we have a few walk-in customers; it is a big event when the UPS man shows up. I often wear slacks and a Hawaiian shirt. However, when I go to meet customers I wear a suit and a tie. It makes me feel professional and that attitude carries over to the meeting with the customer.

In any sales situation it is imperative that you use all the tools that you have to ensure the sales call goes well. Not feeling professional can have the same disastrous affect as not being prepared. This is not an article on how you should dress. We all know when we look and feel professional. To make sales calls without that feeling and confidence about yourself is a disservice to you and your customers. They expect, and should receive, only your best efforts as a professional.

Back to our story, the day after he had talked to the engineer he started wearing a coat and a tie to the studio again. He has been successful for over 50 years and he has been wearing a coat and a tie to work at the broadcast studio every day. Being dressed as a professional gives him a professional feeling about himself and his audience deserves his very best. Larry King's guest was Paul Harvey. "Now you know the rest of the story. Good day."

Action Steps:
- List what you think sets you apart as a professional sales person
- Are you consistently following that list
- What could you do to become more professional
- Set new standards for yourself

> *"In reading the lives of great men, I found that the first victory they won was over themselves . . . self discipline with all of them came first."*
> —Harry S. Truman, U.S. President

Get Organized

Over the years, many systems have been developed to aid sales people in becoming better organized. There are all sorts of computer programs that work well but require dragging along a laptop. The new generation of electronic devices is much smaller and is called PDA (personal data assistant). These both work well and are fun to use until the computer crashes. However, the method that is least expensive, utilizes 3 × 5 note cards. It never crashes or has to boot up. Here is how it works.

On each card list the customer's name, contact person, address, phone and fax number, e-mail address, account number, contract rate, and whatever else you need to know. If you have access to a computer, this data can be printed on label stock and then applied to the card. Here in a simple and an easy format all the information you need is to process an order and get organized. As you prepare for your weekly calls pull the cards of the accounts you want to call on. Now separate the cards by the days of the week. Keep in mind that time not spent in front of the customer is often wasted time. It also means you are not making sales. You will soon be able to arrange your day based not only on the best time to call on the accounts but also with the least amount of driving time.

Just before, you go in for the call, review the card. After each call jot down any significant information. If your customer should happen to mention that they will be celebrating 25 years in business next year, then that is something important. If he or she is not receptive to this week's promotion but would like you to stop with information on an upcoming special section, jot it down. A big help is to keep a list of accounts for special sections. We are not talking about writing paragraphs, just a couple of words to jog your memory. Be sure to write down anything that is a significant personal item, such as a child will be graduating from high school or a wedding is being planned.

As the card gets filled up staple another card to the first card and continue to track the customer. Every year, or at least whenever your company has a rate increase, go back, update the computer list, print new labels, and make new cards. At this time transfer any important information to the new card. As you add new customers add new cards. This is also a great way to keep track of prospective customers as well.

The habit of sending "Thank You" cards is now easy for you to do. Each day select one 3 × 5 card and invest 3 minutes to hand write and address a "Thank You" card to one of your customers. Everything you need to do it is on the customer's card. You have the correct spelling of the name, and the address is right there.

When you return to the office file the customer cards based on the action to be taken. If you are going to contact them, again next week file it for next week's calls. If you are not going to see them for 4 weeks, file it for then. Be sure to list customers who are interested in special sections that you uncovered. Many successful advertising sales people call on their customer at least once a month. So be sure to review each card and schedule a call at least every 30 days. The exciting thing about this method of becoming organized is that you use it the way it works best for you, because if it is not your system then the chance of you using it diminishes greatly.

There you have is a simple system that does not need to be recharged. It never has software problems. It does not require time to boot up. It works when you need it. It fits in your pocket or briefcase. It costs less than $5.00 to set up. With those $5.00 and a few hours of time, you will be on the road to more sales and greater earnings.

Action Steps:

- Choose a method to get organized
- Enter pertinent information
- Update the information daily
- Send a thank you card each day
- Plan and schedule future calls
- Work your plan

"The first part of success is "Get-to-it-iveness;" the second part of success is "Stick-to-it-iveness."
—Orison Swett Marden, Editor, Success Magazine

Hints from the Pros

A few weeks ago, I gave a sales presentation to group of print advertising sales people. Trying to structure a session for an audience that was made up of sales people with a couple of months of experience and some that have been selling print advertising for over 20 years was a real challenge. There is no way that everything could be covered so I chose to highlight several areas that seem to be common threads of Successful Ad Marketers and titled the presentation "SAM."

During the class, those sales people with over 2 years experience were asked to write down advice they would give a new sales person. Below are many of the comments from these seasoned print ad professionals:

1. Be persistent and don't take "No" for an answer. Get down to the bottom of the reason for "No's." Always be positive even if you do get a "No." The next time you call on that person it maybe a "Yes."
2. Set yourself up with a positive attitude. Know your product before you get on the street.

3. Work like you don't need the money! Take every opportunity you get. You never know what you may get out of it.
4. Know your product and make more calls.
5. Smile—be friendly—good attitude—be a partner, not a sales rep. Help their business, your $ will come.
6. Be prepared for each sale. Don't give up. Attitude is more important than skill.
7. Everybody is a prospective friend.
8. Don't sell ads, sell yourself. Customers know the need to advertise. Who they buy it from will be who they like and trust the most.
9. Don't take "no" personally and be yourself.
10. Don't take a turn down personally, see them as opportunities. 80% of sales are made after the fifth sales call.
11. Do what you say you are going to do.
12. Learn the customers' business and spend time and effort to assess their needs.
13. Be confident in yourself, know your product as well as your client and bring a spec ad if you can.
14. Know your product and your customer's needs.
15. Be comfortable, relaxed, and confident. Know your product, and that it will help your customer. Build trust with the customers—let them know you work for them, not for the paper.
16. We are in the business to help other businesses and in the process of helping them you are going to make a difference not only for the business but also for the customer.

17. Neat appearance—keep daily goals checked off as you accomplish them. Be on time.
18. You have not sold someone until they have told you "No."

These are words of wisdom. Each person who submitted a suggestion is a professional ad sales person. Trying to sum up a career to the best advice they can give a new sales person has real value for anyone selling advertising. Whether you are new or not so new in print advertising sales, do yourself a favor and review these hints from the pros every now and then. It is an easy way to stay focused and increase your sales.

Action Steps:

- Focus on one of the ideas at a time and put it into practice
- Try your chosen idea for 30 days and it will become a habit
- Select another idea and practice it for 30 days
- You now have 2 habits to help you increase sales
- Keep going until you have no new ideas to try

"There is no substitute for knowledge."
—W. Edwards Deming

How Well do you Know your Paper?

One of the biggest complaints we hear from potential advertisers is how difficult it is to get information about a paper. When a customer or potential customer calls no one can answer simple questions. To make matters worse, if they leave a number for a call back, there is a good chance no one will, or it will happen too late.

At a seminar a few years ago, the speaker, Tom Zalabak, talked about product knowledge. He devised a "Knowledge Quiz" of things you need to know about your paper in order to communicate with clients. If you cannot answer every question below, then ask your manager, or publisher, for the correct answers. Whether you are an outside or inside sales rep, or the receptionist, these are important questions to know.

Your Paper Quiz.

> How long has your paper been in business?
> What day is you paper delivered to homes?
> Is your paper audited?
> Can I run a reverse ad?
> Can I run my ad upside down?
> What is your classified ad rate?
> What is the classified deadline?

Can I send my ad by e-mail? If so, how?
Why should I put prices on items in the ad?
What are your page dimensions?
Do you use SAUs? If not, what is your column width?
Which should I use in my ad this photo or this drawing?
What are the rules regarding inserts?
What is the cost for a single sheet 8.5 inch by 11 inch insert?
Where do I send my inserts?
Is there a discount if I pay in advance?
Is there a discount for "camera ready ads"?
What is your local open rate?
Is that rate commissionable or non-commissionable?
Do you offer contact rates?
Do you offer frequency discounts? If so, what are the discounts?
What is your deadline for display ads?
Do you send tearsheets?
How much is spot color?
How much is process color?
What is your deadline for inserts?
What is the busiest month of the year for your top advertiser?
What is the slowest month of the year for your top advertiser?
Who is your top advertiser's biggest competitor?
How many locations does your top advertiser have?
How many locations does your top advertiser's competitor have?
Where else does your top advertiser advertise now?

There are most likely other questions that people want to know. A great sales meeting might be to go over this list, add some more questions, and then answer them.

Distribute the answered questions to all the people who make customer contact. Remember to update the answers as you have rate increases and circumstances change.

Action Steps:
- Seek answers to all the questions above
- Add more questions and answers that are needed
- Distribute the answered questions to anyone who has customer contact
- Be sure to update as information changes

"Go out on a limb—that's where the fruit is."
—Will Rogers, Humorist

I was Once "THE KING"!

Have you ever done something and later could not believe what happened? Was it so out of character that you were red faced and embarrassed for several hours afterwards? Years later people remember the incident, bring it up, and you have to relive it yet again. Since people in our industry like to help each other, you can learn a valuable lesson at my expense.

First of all, if your association has a hypnotist for the entertainment, think twice before you volunteer to be a subject. This is especially true if you know you can be hypnotized. You will get a great deal of encouragement from your so-called friends. THIS MAY BE A MISTAKE!

My life changed, 12 years ago, when I walked on the stage and in less than a minute, I was under the hypnotist's spell. The easy part was believing that I was at a horse race and my shoes were binoculars. As the hypnotist called the race, my shoes were held up to my eyes and followed the horses around the track. My horse lost as usual. Next, he told me that I was a phenomenon of modern medicine and was the first male to be pregnant. As he took me through the first few months, I was sure that I was beginning to show and could not find a comfortable sitting position no matter how hard I tried. Then, he wanted to know what my wife was going to say about my condition. I had no clue how to tell her, but I knew she would not be too happy. You will be glad to know that the birth went well and father and child are doing fine.

What could be worse? Let me tell you. I was convinced that I was THE KING. At this point in my hypnotic trance, I was told to sing "Jail House Rock" with my make-believe guitar and with all of the hip gyrations that are a meaningful part of being Elvis. As the music played and I went into my routine, people in the audience began to laugh. They had tears running down their cheeks. My dear wife was holding her side because it hurt so much. People from other meetings, in other parts of the hotel, ran in to see what could cause such a thunderous audience reaction. I must have been a huge success because after all these years people from our association still call me Elvis. They still talk about my performance and smile and laugh. Pictures still appear in the association's newsletter.

What does this have to do with our industry and sales? (Some of the best sales training is found at your association's conferences and meetings.) It is called getting involved. It is doing whatever is necessary to help your association. My being Elvis for 10 minutes has given me many additional friends and acquaintances in the industry. Your association can use your help, guidance, leadership, and support. Next time raise your hand. Volunteer! If the worst that can happen to you is that you sing "Jail House Rock" just like Elvis, (with all the movements) then you too will be blessed with friends and fond memories of your fellow members in the industry having a great time.

We all believe in the power of ELVIS, because each letter in that name refers to values that we in the industry all hold so dear.

- **E**thical business is our only business
- **L**earning from each other is priceless
- **V**olunteer to help your association and fellow members
- **I**nvest in your customers, your paper, and your association
- **S**upport each other and grow

I am somewhat proud of my rendition of THE KING's classic recording, but I am ecstatic about our industry, its people, and our future. Get involved!

Action Steps:

- Attend your association meetings
- Be willing to invest personal time to improve your career
- Join committees, help out, and get involved
- Never stop learning about your profession

"When you walk what you talk . . . people listen."
—Anonymous

In Need of Training

I just received an e-mail from a reader who wanted information about getting additional sales training. The person had been selling print advertising for less than a year and stated that she did not receive much training when she started. She wanted to know if I had any suggestions.

One of the success factors of a sales person is to continue to train and seek training. Most sales people do not want to spend their money, or at least not very much of their money, for training. Where can a person go to get sales training and not spend much money? There are several ways to accomplish both objectives.

How about weekly training for about $60.00 a year? That figures out to just over $1.00 a week. The necessary training is available at your local Toastmasters Club. Most of these clubs meet for an hour each week and have a structured meeting planned, conducted, and presented by the individual members. It is an organization that trains people how to speak and communicate effectively. They train people how to prepare, how to be leaders, how to be confident, and how to be professional.

After the beginning course, which everyone uses, there is an actual course on selling.

Is your sales career worth an investment of $60.00? Will you be nervous when you give your first speech at a Toastmaster Meeting? The answer is "yes". Will you overcome that fear? Again the answer is "yes". But, if you do not try something new to improve yourself you will always be what you are now. For information about Toastmasters visit their web site at **www.toastmasters.org**. This web site contains all the information you need to find a club and learn about Toastmasters.

The next suggestion is to find out what associations your publication belongs to. Your sales manager or publisher can give you this information. E-mail or call the association and ask about conferences or meetings where there will be sales training. Often the cost to attend is relatively small. At almost every conference there is an emphasis on sales training. Ask your publisher if you can go. Then, offer to attend on your time. Many of the conferences are in a central location that makes driving the best way to get there.

Each association does their best to hire trainers and speakers that can best suit the needs of the members. Sales people can learn about effective copy writing that works, ads that should not run, how to plan, and new sales techniques. Each association has meetings or sessions that are geared toward sales.

Many of these same associations have lending libraries that have books, audio tapes, video tapes, and DVDs that are free or almost free to check out. Some of the nation's best sales trainers can be found this way. The public library may have the sales training material that is needed.

One of the best sales training techniques is to ride along and shadow a successful sales rep. Most reps are willing to do this because they all started out and needed help. The sales manager may be willing to ride along with a new sales person and critique the sales call shortly after it is completed. Both of these opportunities allow for a genuine sales experience in front of an actual customer. It is a super way to learn and can expose the sales person to training that is in a sense customized for the paper.

The sales person who wants additional training can certainly find it in a variety of ways. The commitment is to the time involved. A sales person who makes such a commitment will reap the rewards with increased sales and earnings. All the training sessions and materials are ready for the sales person who is ready to make such a commitment.

Action Steps:

- Check out a Toastmasters' meeting near you.
- Find out which associations your paper is a member
- Be willing to invest your time for improvement
- Always have a book, article, tape, or CD for when you have extra time
- Always seek improvement

> *"Opportunity is missed by most people because it is dressed in overalls and looks like work."*
> —Thomas Edison, Inventor

Is a Computer the Answer?

Remembering back to my first computer, I was able to go online and spend hours searching for information and even more time trying to see how this computer would help me do my job better. Those first few months were some of the lowest productivity months of my sales career. I had never worked harder or worked more hours. Hour upon hour was invested making my presentation just right. All sorts of statistics were right there on the computer screen. There were records about everything that was part of my job.

All of this was great and fun. However, my job performance started to slip. It was easy to rationalize; all I had to do is tell myself that I was busy working on this proposal or that spreadsheet. After all, look at all the time that had been spent collecting this data or writing this proposal. To confirm all of the activity, just look at the piles of computer printed reports and notebooks full of computer printouts.

During this phase, the most important thing in sales was forgotten. The contacts were not being made. Sure, the people who had expressed interest in my products and were in the pipeline, ready to close, were contacted. I even was the sales leader the 2nd month of computer ownership. With that recognition the logical conclusion was the computer made all those sales possible.

The next month was just "so so" as far as my sales went. However, the amount of data that was in the computer was mind-boggling. The 3rd month was not so hot. The 4th month was the worst since being a rooky sales person. There was no one to call on and sell my products to. Where were all those people? The first thought was that the industry was just depressed. After all, I had the best data available and was a past sales leader.

Then my boss sat me down and started asking questions about what was being done differently. The computer was the one thing that was monopolizing so much time. Neglecting the businesses that were going to provide sales in the future had shut down the flow of new sales contacts. There were zero prospects. This meant starting at ground zero and building the business again. It was not easy and did not happen over night.

The next month was dismal for sales but outstanding on cold calls and customer contacts. The month after the sales picked up and the cold calls and customer contacts stayed up. By the 4th month I was again back as one of the top producers. Selling time on the street was divided into thirds. A third was devoted to cold calling, a third was follow up customer contacts, and a third was giving presentations and closing sales. Only after the day was done on the street did the computer get turned on.

The computer became a tool to help keep track of customers and help write proposals. I no longer fooled myself by spending time trying to have the most data or the most up to date industry projections. Days were busy cold calling, contacting customers, and closing sales.

It is easy to get side tracked into thinking that a computer will solve all your problems. However, a computer will not do the one thing necessary to make sales. It cannot make personal contacts for you. It cannot make the cold calls, do the presentations, or close the sale. The computer can be an asset in helping to make you more productive and organized. To be a sales leader, you need to maximize the time in front of the customer and prospective customers during selling hours and use other time for the computer.

Action Steps:
- Be aware of time-wasting activities
- Use selling time to be in front of customers
- Always make cold calls to keep the pipeline full
- Use your computer to assist your selling time

"People who are unable to motivate themselves must be content with mediocrity."
—Andrew Carnegie, Industrialist

It Costs More Not to Attend!

Your state, regional, or national association host meetings during the year designed to help you and the rest of your paper's staff to become more proficient at your jobs. With most small paper operations you do not have the time or the budget to conduct the necessary training to help your people succeed. That is where the association really shines. They bring in the experts to train. Most of the time the meetings are held at convenient locations and times so the various staff members can attend. The sessions are not tied together, so if people cannot attend all of the conference, they can still get the training they need by attending the portion that is of most interest to them.

How much does it cost? Not much when you consider that there is little or no registration fee or charges for meals. The best part—the fellowship with other industry people is absolutely an added benefit that is provided without charge. That leaves the hotel room, which in most cases is at a reduced rate or brought down and transportation to and from the meeting. In the end, the out-of-pocket cost is minimal.

If attendance to the association's conferences is used as a reward for exceptional job performance, everybody wins. First of all, the employee(s) gets to go and secondly they receive valuable training while they are at the conference to take back to the paper and share with their fellow employees. This concept is a true "win—win" reward program. Employees are rewarded by going to a conference where they associate with people who have the same interests. At these association meetings everyone is interested in papers. They all want to know the best way to do their job and they are willing to share ideas with their peers. The publication wins because it is providing recognition, training, and job loyalty all at the same time.

The true cost for the publication is the opportunity cost that is lost because the paper's people did not attend. It is the cost of lost revenue because the sales people did not get the training that would help them sell additional ads. They did not learn the secret of selling an ad series. They did not learn how to ask the questions that lead to sales. It is the cost of missing out on really great promotional ideas because no one attended the meeting to learn about the opportunities. It is the extra cost incurred because the composition people did not go to the meeting and learn those time-saving tricks with PhotoShop. It is the lost revenue because no one from the paper attended the meeting on how to hire people.

Some do not attend because of the time commitment. But that is most likely an excuse. It is more a situation of setting priorities. You need to evaluate the actual benefit as compared to the true cost. Once that is done, the decision to become involved in your association(s) and attend the meetings makes sound financial sense. The most successful papers attend association meeting because the cost of not attending the association conferences is far greater than the cost of attending. Think about it.

Action Steps:
- Find out when your association(s) has meetings
- Asked to be put on the mailing list for conference information
- Be willing to invest your time to attend a conference
- Attend as many sessions as possible at the conference
- Come prepared to share ideas

"In good times, people want to advertise; in bad times, they have to."
—Bruce Barton

It is a Numbers Game

A study by the US government reported people retain only 10% of what they read. Is it any wonder that when a sales person drops off information about an upcoming promotion at a potential customer's place of business the chance of making a sale is slim to none? The potential advertiser who might read the material will only remember 10% of what they read. That is a long way from a sales call. Prospecting and selling advertising with that approach is like playing the lottery.

When the ad sales person is in front of the customer and able to tell the potential customer about the promotion, that person will retain only 20% of the information. If they can see a handout or a sample, while being told about the promotion the customer will retain 50% of the information. Being able to see something adds 30% more than if they just hear the information. It is no wonder when a sales person goes into a customer's business and is prepared with something tangible in hand the success rate of closing the sale goes way up.

The experienced sales people will engage the customer in a conversation about the upcoming promotion because they know if they can tell the story and the customer can see a sample they are at a 50% retention level. With the customers involvement in the conversation the retention jumps to 70%. At 70% the chance of closing is extremely high.

To get to 90% retention the sales people must get the customer actively involved. They need to have the customer take some sort of action that shows ownership. That can be accomplished by being prepared with a spec ad that is not quite complete. The customer needs to help in some way to finish the ad. It may be in the proper placing and size of the logo. It may be in the pricing of the items listed. It could be as simple as having to enlarge the store hours on the ad. Once the customer is doing something to the ad, it is his or her ad. The sale is almost certain.

We often hear that "sales" is just a numbers game. If you make enough calls, someone will buy. In a way it really is a numbers game, but the numbers that are important are the numbers that really make a difference and they are:

- 10% of what they read
- 20% of what they hear
- 30% of what they see
- 50% of what they see and hear
- 70% of what they say
- 90% of what they say and do

Getting the customer involved in the sales process is what makes the difference. The more involved they are the higher the closing ratio. Successful ad sales people play the numbers game only if they know which numbers lead to sales.

Action Steps:

- Be prepared for each sales call
- Always have something to show the customer that you can leave with them
- Ask open-ended questions to gain buy in
- Use spec ads to get the customer involved
- Be prepared for increased sales

> "Luck is a dividend of sweat. The more you sweat, the luckier you get."
>
> —Ray Kroc

It is not Luck

Recently, I was asked, "What is the single most important thing print advertising sales people need to know in order to be successful?" The question posed a real challenge for me. So many things help make them successful. There is product knowledge, selling skills, time management, desire, listening skills, honesty, organizational skills, planning, goal setting, and others. The more the question was pondered the more the same answer kept coming to the top. There is a direct correlation between being successful and the amount of work that is done. There it is in one word—"work." To be successful you have to work.

Every so often you will hear that sales people are successful because they are lucky. That is not true. The successful sales person makes his or her own luck by doing the work in order to succeed. Have you ever heard that luck is 10% inspiration and 90% perspiration? That big sale that your team mate just sold was not because of luck. It was a result of the amount of work that was done to make the sale. It was the amount of work that was done in order for them to realize there was an opportunity.

Sometimes you hear that a sales person is successful because he or she "works smart." What is working smart? It is using your time, knowledge, selling skills, planning, and more to best serve the customer. It is taking care of the customer because that, in turn, allows the customer to take care of you. It means being organized and calling on customers because you have an appointment. It means spending the extra time to be prepared for the call. It means establishing a working relationship with your customers so you are viewed as a part of the marketing team.

In the chapter about what successful sales people do, if you go back and review that list again you will find that, in every example, the successful sales person was working more and working smarter. No one suggested that you need to stay in the office and wait for the customers to come to you. No one suggested that you come to work a little later or leave a little earlier. To me it seems quite simple. If you need to make 10% more this year, and you do not change anything about how you sell, then you need to spend 10% more time doing what you do. Working smarter allows you to add that 10% more by becoming more efficient. It means that you put forth the effort to become better at your profession.

Work is not spending hours in front of your computer establishing an impressive database about your customers. That is "feel good" busy work. It is "feel good" because it is so easy to convince yourself that you are working. You will actually go home at night and be tired. You will have a sense of accomplishment when the project is done. What you will not have are sales. The database you just developed will not make a single sales call. That only happens when you make the sales call. Over time it is easy to find various "feel good" projects that will not lead to your success. The time to devote to things that may help you become a sales success is outside of selling time.

It all comes down to work. You have to be willing to put forth the effort to be the very best you can. You need to seek out training to improve your skills. You need to set realistic goals. You need to devote the time to take care of the customer and become a part of the marketing team. If you want to be a success, luck will not cut it. Ray Kroc, founder of McDonalds, said it best, "Luck is a dividend of sweat. The more you sweat, the luckier you get."

Action Steps:

- Analyze how you work now checking for time wasters
- Evaluate what you need to change
- Be prepared to work more hours
- Learn to work smart
- Enjoy your success

"If you fail to plan . . . you are planning to fail."
—Anonymous

It is Planning Season

It is always the right time to plan for your success for the next 12 months. Your manager most likely has told you what is expected from you as far as a sales goal. You have some what started developing a plan in your head but that is about as far as it has gone. I could tell you how important it is to plan and that without well-defined written goals your chance of success is less than 2%. If the goal is your manager's goal and not your goal the chance for success is even less. None of this is new, yet only 2% of the print advertising sales people will bother to establish personal, written, and meaningful sales goals. Then in the last quarter of the year they are wondering why. Maybe investing a few hours of your time is not worth being successful.

Here is a new and refreshing idea. Why not do a strategic plan using SWOT analysis about you? That is right—you. It works for small businesses, large corporations, associations, and organizations. It can work for you. SWOT stands for "Strengths," "Weaknesses," "Opportunities," and "Threats."

Take out a sheet of paper. On the top write "Strengths." Start listing all of your strengths. Be honest and fair. It may go something like this:

>   Honest
>   Hardworking
>   Dedicated
>   Creative
>   Punctual
>   Fair
>   Intelligent
>   Willing to learn
>   Spend 30 minutes doing this and come up with at least 25 things.

Do the same exercise for "Weaknesses." Again, be honest and fair to yourself. For example:

>   Not goal oriented
>   Suffer call reluctance
>   Procrastinate
>   Overly optimistic
>   Lack of sale skills
>   Get bogged down with busy work
>   Not professional enough
>   Again, spend 30 minutes and come up with 25 things.

Continue doing the exercise for "Opportunities." Your list may start something like this:

>   Call on new businesses
>   Use spec ads
>   Offer solutions to problems
>   Be a sales person, not an order taker

Develop meaningful personal goals
Use time wisely
Track calls by number and type
Plan the next week before leaving on Friday
Spend 30 minutes and set a goal of 25 items

"Threats" will be handled the same way. The list might start like this:

- Competition
  - Radio
  - TV
  - Internet
  - Cable
  - Phone book
- Economy
  - Super store coming to town
  - Not getting sales training
  - Newsprint prices
  - Postage costs

Write down 25 things and allow 30 minutes to do this.

As you look over each of the 4 sheets of 25 or more items you will start to see common themes that reappear on the lists. For example, the lists above show that the person needs additional sales training. They also need help in planning and goal setting. Education in time management is also detected. With a list of 25 items on each page there will be several other themes that stand out. You need to select the 3 or 4 most important and set dates as to when you are going to do something about the selected themes. If it is additional sales training, you need to plan step-by-step how you are going to get that accomplished. Then write it down, post it, and tell people what you are going to do as a result of your personal strategic plan. Now you are committed to do something that will improve you. Review your plan often so you stay on track. Do the same thing for the other themes selected.

Next year do another strategic plan and follow your plan. Planning is the key, without it you have no idea where you are going. You move but have no sense of direction. You work but have little results. Without a plan you are working your way toward failure. Now is the planning season.

Action Steps:

- Set aside up to 4 hours of time to do your personal strategic plan
- Be sure you are free from distractions
- Be honest and fair to yourself
- Select 3 or 4 themes you want to work on
- Develop an action plan and a time frame to complete the task
- Reward yourself as you complete each task

> "Tell me and I will forget, Show me and I will remember, Involve me and I will understand."
> —Confucius

Just a Reminder

I was talking to a major media buyer the other day and he made the comment that even when he tells sales people that they should do a needs analysis to find out how their paper can help solve a problem for a particular advertiser, no one ever does the needs analysis. The typical sales people just start in telling about their publication. They have all the facts and figures down and share the information willingly. The result is no sale. They walk away wondering "why." After all, their paper is the best in the market place and they told the media buyer everything they needed to make the only logical buying decision.

As a sales person, remember this line, "Tell me and I will forget." It is not too hard to understand. Has someone asked you to pick something up after work and it totally slipped your mind? Your customers are the same as you. When you just tell your story, or sales pitch, it is soon forgotten.

The quote goes on "Show me and I will remember." The very act of having something to show your customer helps them to remember. When explaining about your paper it is helpful to have a presentation notebook so you can show the customer your audit results, distribution area, testimonials, or special section. Not only does this help the customer remember, it also helps you remember. It allows for a smooth transition from one topic to the next. The sales person acts like a professional when he or she is organized. That will happen with a presentation notebook or folder.

The customer will have a visual representation of what you are saying and is more likely to remember. Think about it. If you were able to offer a map that showed your distribution area by zip code, would that leave an impression? What if you could overlay the customer's store location(s) on top of your distribution map? Being able to show the customer what you are describing makes a big difference in getting the sale.

What about the needs analysis? The last of the quote is "Involve me and I will understand." If you take the time to do a needs analysis you will have the customer involved in the sales process. You are asking them what will make their job easier. What are some of the problems in their current advertising program? What would you like to see from a new media or a paper? When you find out their needs then you are able to demonstrate how your paper can fill those needs. You are now a partner with your advertiser. You are working to solve their problems and not just to make a sale. You now have a relationship with the customer.

All of this wisdom is not new. It was around for years and years. From time to time we need to be reminded.

Action Steps:

- Develop a list of open questions to ask potential customers
- Enlist the help of your manager
- When talking to a potential customer, ask if they would mind helping you to understand their needs then ask your questions
- Come back at another time to explain and show your ideas and plans to the prospect

"We miss 100 percent of the sales we don't ask for."
—Zig Ziglar

"No" Is Almost as Good as "Yes"

Closing is the most feared part of the sales process. Although, it is the natural progression of the events and conversations that have gone on up to that point. Closing requires that the sales person has confidence and courage. Confidence comes from the knowledge that you have about your paper. The better you understand the rate card, the media kit, the audit, and the readership study the more confidence you will have. Courage is needed to over come the fear of rejection. We fear rejection because we think we have failed and therefore, we are a failure. You must remember that failure is an event and not a person.

There is no set time to close a sale. It can happen at the beginning, an end, or anywhere in between. By asking questions during the sales process the closing can take place at any time during the sales call. Ask questions such as:

- Does this fit your advertising plans?
- Should I go over the rate information with you?
- Would you like to use color in your ad?

This technique is often called a trial close. However, if you are at the end of your presentation and have not closed, ask for the order. Your customer knows why you are there and he or she is expecting you to ask for a commitment.

Closing the sale is a test of your success. It is natural to feel uptight and nervous. If the customer says "yes" then you make more money, your paper makes money, and your boss is happy. At the closing stage "the pressure is on." Moreover, we feel that stress. On the other side, your customer can sense what you are feeling. Now think about it. You have done everything. You have followed all the steps of the sale. So, why not feel relaxed and confident. If the answer is "no," it is not because of you, but because of something else. You have not failed. If the answer is "no", you must clear up any misunderstandings. This happens often because we assume our customer understood everything we said. The customer said "no" to get additional information or to get something cleared up. Next you should reinforce the benefits and overcome any objections. At this point you have every right to ask for the order again. The sales person who always accepts an uncontested "no" for the first answer is not going to be successful in selling advertising.

When prospecting for new accounts, advertising sales people will often get a "no" and then classify that business as a non-advertiser and never call on them again. The sales person will soon believe that that person is a jerk who knows nothing about advertising. Would you be receptive to spending money with someone you do not know and had never met before, who just showed up at your front door? I would hope not. So, why should the person you prospected for the first time buy on the first call?

Here is an interesting bit of research. Of those sales people prospecting for new accounts:

- 44% give up after 1 "no" and never go back
- 22% give up after 2 "no's" and never go back
- 14% give up after 3 "no's" and never go back
- 12% give up after 4 "no's" and never go back
- 8% ask 5 or more times

Sixty percent of all customers say "no" 4 times before saying "yes!" Remember a "no" does not mean that you are a failure. Failure is an event and not a person. Learning to accept "no" as a step in the sales process will let you be one of the 8% who go back 5 or more times. Learning to accept "no" will also help you get more sales from existing customers.

Action Steps:

- Make a list of potential customers that you stopped contacting
- Sort the list starting with the prospects you feel are easiest to convert into customers
- Develop a plan to systematically call on these prospects
- On every call ask for the order
- Do not give up contacting these prospects until you have made 5 or more calls
- Keep accurate records of the calls made to each prospect

"If you find a path with no obstacles, it probably doesn't lead anywhere."
—Frank A. Clark

Not an Objection!

Do you cringe when you are at the end of your sales presentation and you ask for the order and hear an objection? Do you feel uncomfortable or have doubts that you are doing a good job of selling? Do you ever wish there was an easy way to handle objections? If you are like most sales people the answer is "yes" to all 3 questions. Sales people tend to feel that an objection is a personal attack. What is actually happening is the customer is asking for additional information or clarification of something that was said. There is no personal attack.

The way you handle the objection can make or break the success of the sale. First restate the objection. This is done so you are both talking about the same thing. If the customer said that your paper was too expensive, you restate that objection. It is as simple as saying, "Mr. Jones you think our paper is too expensive. Is that correct?" When you have agreement you now must answer the objection.

It is easy to respond with an honest answer and be 100% correct yet sound confrontational to the customer. No one likes to be told that they are wrong. Therefore, the salesperson must soften the way the objection is answered. There needs to be a certain amount of empathy toward the customer. Now is the time to be a salesperson and take control of the call.

Every one has heard about the "feel, felt, found" response. The reason we have heard about it is because it works. For an example, the customer might say that your paper is too expensive. Instead of saying "you are wrong" you say, "Mr. Jones. I know how you feel. I had other clients who felt the same way. However, when we compared total circulation and readership they found our cost to reach a single client was half the cost of the XYZ Paper."

At a recent seminar the speaker totally dismissed the "feel, felt, found" answer because she thought it was over used. If you think that way of answering objections is over used then rephrase it in to something more acceptable to you. Do not make the mistake of not using a method that results in a significant higher closing ratio. How about, "Mr. Jones I understand where you are coming from. As a matter of fact, some of my best advertisers had the same idea about my paper. But, when we calculated the cost to reach one customer our rates were substantially lower."

Or you could say, "Mr. Jones you are correct when you compare total dollar amounts. However, our advertisers have discovered that was not the complete story. Their analysis revealed that when you compare the cost to reach a single customer that my paper was actually a substantial cost savings."

Here is a sure fire way to answer the objection and gain credibility at the same time. Use a third party in your response. In response to the example you might say, "Mr. Jones, I know how you feel. Bob Smith at Smith Auto felt the same way. However, he found out that reaching more customers at a lower cost per customer translated into increased auto sales and lower selling costs per unit." It only works if what you are saying is true.

The other way is the "yes, but" response. Using the same example as above the response would be something like this: "Yes, Mr. Jones we cost more than the XYZ Paper, but when you compare our larger circulation and the cost to reach a single customer we are 50% less."

Now ask for the order again. (Closing the sale is a topic in itself.) Practice one of these techniques until it is comfortable for you to respond naturally. Think back to the objections you have received in the past and write answers to those objections. With a little practice you will be handling objection without fear.

Remember to restate the objection, use a method that allows you to be empathetic with the customer and yet have control of the sales process, and ask for the order again. You will have earned it.

Action Steps:

- Develop a positive attitude about objections
- Become comfortable with a way to answer objections without being confrontational
- Make a list of your most common objections
- Practice your response to those objections
- Enjoy increased sales and income

"The only thing that stands between a person and what they want in life is often the will to try it and the faith to believe it's possible."
—Rich Devos

Now is the Time

At the end of the year and after you have enjoyed the holidays, take a few minutes to reflect back over the past year and recall some of the things that you wanted to accomplish but did not. Now take a few minutes to analyze why.

Author and motivational speaker, Brian Tracy puts it into perspective when he states that if you ask 100 people if they have goals, 90% will raise their hand. I am sure that each and every one of you would be there with hands raised. We all have goals. We know what we want to accomplish. We are proud to tell others that we have goals. But, here we are, starting the New Year and we have not accomplished what we set out to achieve a year ago. Does this sound familiar?

Next, Brian Tracy asks how many people have their goals written down? Only 10 hands are stilled raised. This 10% are the people who are on top. They make the most money and they enjoy life. Some of you have your hand in the air but you have not accomplished all that you wanted to last year. Certainly, nothing like what you had in mind a year ago. Things did not seem to click for you on achieving your goals. Your sales are up or you are able to accomplish your job with more skill and knowledge but the end result was a far cry from your original goals. Somewhere along the line things seemed to stall.

"Will the people who have their goals written down and well planned out on how to achieve those goals please keep their hands raised?" Now we have only 2 people with hands in the air. Guess what, these people "the 2 percenters" are the people who are the super stars in their jobs. Everything with their personal life is in place. They tend to be envied by the other 98%. This all happens because they had goals that were written down and well-planned out.

Would you start a trip across the United States without a map? Without that map you may know where you want to go, but not have a clue how to get there. If you took some time before you left on the trip, you could plan where you wanted to stop each night. You would plan for the best routes. You would plan to make the trip an efficient use of your time. You would not just start out and head for the setting sun. The same is true of your goals. Without a plan you work aimlessly trying to hit your goal.

If you decide to join this elite group of the most successful people, "the 2 percenters," here are a few things you should know. You will increase your income by at least 15% the first year. You will be looked up to as a person that is going places. You will be asked to be a leader. You will enjoy your job. You will feel fulfilled. You will find new energy you never knew existed. Your personal life will improve. You will become proactive instead of reactive.

Take the time to set goals so that you are part of the top 2%. Make an investment in yourself. After all, the return is far greater than any other investment. For a few hours of your time you will reap the rewards. There is plenty of room at the top. Even after reading this only 2% of you will invest in yourself and become a super star. Your first goal should be to become one of the 2%. Now write it down. Next spend some time planning how to get there. Remember: "If you fail to plan, then you plan to fail."

Action Steps:

- Set aside half a day to work on your goals
- Formulate a detailed plan of action
- Write it down
- Review your plan weekly and stay focused
- Make goal setting an annual event
- Welcome to "the 2 percenters"

"Success is a journey, not a destination."
—Anonymous

Once is not Enough—How Often Should you Advertise?

We all know that ad frequency is an important element in a successful advertising campaign or promotion. What are readers actually thinking as they read an ad in your paper? Back in 1885 Thomas Smith, a nineteenth century London businessman, offered the following advice to advertisers. It is still applicable today:

1. The first time people look at any given ad; they do not even see it.
2. The second time, they do not notice it.
3. The third time, they are aware that it is there.
4. The fourth time, they have a fleeting sense that they have seen it somewhere before.
5. The fifth time, they actually read the ad.
6. The sixth time, they thumb their nose at it.
7. The seventh time, they start to get a little irritated at it.
8. The eighth time, they start to think, "Here is that confound ad again."
9. The ninth time, they start to wonder if they may be missing out on something.

10. The tenth time, they ask their friends and neighbors if they have tried it.
11. The eleventh time, they wonder how the company is paying for all these ads.
12. The twelfth time, they start to think that it must be a good product.
13. The thirteenth time, they start to feel the product has value.
14. The fourteenth time, they start to remember wanting a product exactly like this for a long time.
15. The fifteenth time, they start to yearn for it because they cannot afford to buy it.
16. The sixteenth time, they accept the fact that they will buy it sometime in the future.
17. The seventeenth time, they make a note to buy the product.
18. The eighteenth time, they curse their poverty for not allowing them to buy this terrific product.
19. The nineteenth time, they count their money very carefully.
20. The twentieth time prospects see the ad; they buy what is being offered.

What this really means, if advertisers are not seeing the results from their advertising campaign in 6 weeks, they should not give up hope! Now take a few minutes and think about those advertisers who run with you every week. Their ad may not be one of the largest but week in and week out their ad is in your paper. They are there each week when the economy is strong and when it is weak. These knowledgeable advertisers have discovered the secret of consistent and frequent advertising. They are the lifeblood of your paper.

Action Steps:

- Make a copy of the list to give to your customers
- Make a list of advertisers that run each week to use as examples
- Encourage your advertisers to become consistent with their advertising
- Become part of the solution for your customers

> *"Practice does not make perfect, perfect practice makes perfect."*
>
> —Vince Lombardi

Practice Makes Money

The other day, I started thinking about professional athletes. The thoughts were about how much time they must train to become proficient at their chosen sport. Years ago we attended a national golf tournament in the area. What struck me the most was early in the morning and late at night there were professional golfers on the driving range. They were not just hitting a bucket of balls. They were hitting numerous buckets of balls. They put in all that work in hopes of cutting a stroke or two from their game. Next they would spend hours putting.

Baseball, basketball, football, tennis, track, and all the other sports require the athlete to spend most of their time practicing. They practice to become a little better next time they play the game. These are the professional athletes that we all admire. As a sales person you are a professional. How much time do you give to practicing? If you are the typical sales person the answer is "very little". We all know that we have to practice to become good at anything. Yet, when it comes to our occupation of selling we think that we do not need to practice. Do we honestly think that we are that good?

Many sales organizations require their sales people to get constant training and often practice their sales calls. When I had to do it I always became nervous. What would I do if I embarrassed myself in front of the boss? What if I forgot one of the selling steps? What would the rest of the sales department think of me? Looking back that was some of the best training I ever received. Making a mistake in front of the other sales people did not cost me any money. Making a mistake with a client could cost me dearly.

First of all, there are several ways to practice. Role playing always comes to mind. This is by far the best. Not only are you practicing your sales skills, you get instant feed back from your boss and the rest of the team. The main reason we do not want to role play is because it makes us nervous. Get over it. It makes everyone nervous. Role playing is a win, win, win for everyone. You win because you learn. Your fellow sales people win because they learn. Your customer wins because you are more professional. Nobody loses from role playing. Think about it.

Another way to practice is to make a sales call and right after the call evaluate what you did right and what you did wrong. You can do this yourself with a notebook to write down notes about the last call. At the end of the day you have a complete record of what transpired. Whenever I had someone ride with me I would ask them to evaluate my last sales call as we drove to the next call. That way I got instant feed back so I would not make the same mistake on the next call. When I was asked to ride with a sales person we always evaluated each call right after the call.

Another great way to practice is to join Toastmasters. There is one in your community and the cost is minimal. The first part of Toastmasters allows you to overcome being so nervous when speaking in front of other people. It is also a great way to practice giving a presentation. After the first introduction series there is the option to select a more advanced series and the one I would recommend to sales people is the course on selling. This would be a great way to practice and to learn about your chosen profession.

A final way to practice is to visualize. This does not replace actual practicing, but it does make you sharp and ready for your sales call. When a runner is starting a race, that person will spend a few seconds visualizing the entire race including winning. The professional sales person also visualizes the sales call from start to finish and making the sale. They know that their chance of making the sale is greatly increased by visualizing. When they give a presentation they expect to make the sale. Their attitude is one of winning. Consequently, they go into the sales call mentally ahead of all the other sales people.

Remember, practice does make perfect and it makes you money. There is no other way than to practice your self to riches. All successful people practice—including successful sales people.

Action Steps:

- Decide to become a true professional and practice
- Ask your manager if part of the sales meeting could be devoted to role playing
- Evaluate the good and bad of every sales call
- Always be prepared for your sales calls
- Visualize just before you go into an appointment
- Enjoy your success

> *"We are all faced with a series of great opportunities brilliantly disguised as impossible situations."*
> —Chuck Swindoll

Prejudge and Lose

Sales people will often prejudge a potential customer by the type of business, or the appearance of the business building, and make a mental note to the effect that the business does not advertise. Month in and month out the sales person just drives by the business and never stops to learn anything about it. This is a huge mistake. It is huge in that the sales person made the decision for the customer that they would not advertise in the paper. The sad thing is the sales person is right. The customer was never given a chance.

Customers come in all shapes and sizes. It is impossible to determine a potential customer's needs by just driving by. Likewise, the condition of the facility does not really tell much.

My first job right out of college was a stock broker for a large company in downtown Chicago. One day a man walked into the office wearing bib overalls scuffed work boots and carrying an old dilapidated gym bag. He went to the receptionist and said he wanted information about a bond offering. Each day the office assigns a broker to be broker of the day. That person gets to work with all walk in traffic. The broker of the day took one look at the man and told a brand new broker to take care of the man. This young broker's desk was close to mine. I thought to myself, "What a waste of time this guy will be."

I could hear most of what was being said. The man said he had seen the announcement in the paper that our company was part of the underwriting group for some municipal bonds. The young broker was pleasant and explained the value of municipal bonds is that the interest is federally tax free. The man said he knew that and wanted 125 of the bonds. The broker explained that the bonds were offered at 99 meaning $990.00 each and that 125 of them would cost over $123,000.00. The man said he was aware of that and said he wanted 125 bonds. The next question the broker asked was "How do you want to pay for this?"

He responded, "You take cash, don't you?" with that, he started pulling $100 bills out of the gym bag. The office was locked down and the man and his money were taken to the cash gage. The broker's commission was $30 per bond or $3750.00.

A few years ago, I received a call from a company that buys furs from hunters and trappers around the state. I was given an address in a small rural town and a time and date to meet. I arrived in the town early which was a good thing as I was totally lost. After stopping at a gas station for directions, I was soon driving down a dirt road looking for a dilapidated building and a sign that said something about fur. Ten minutes later I was at my destination. I almost left but remembering the lesson learned years ago, I went in. I thought the outside was bad. The inside was worse. The person I was to meet came up to me and asked if he could show me around. I have never seen so many traps, pelts, and guns in one place in my life.

We got down to business and he wanted to run ads in 23 different towns. I was able to place the order and send out the ads to the papers. The customer was quite pleased with the results and paid promptly. That was 7 years ago and the same company is still running the ads with us every autumn. Had I prejudged this business, I would never have stopped to see if they needed help with their advertising. If I allowed my judgmental feelings to take control, I would have never opened the door of my car and made the call.

Over the years we have all prejudged businesses and have never tried to contact them about their advertising needs. If you would invest a little time to just stop in and find out what sort of business these potential customers operate, you would learn a great deal about your community and you will find some hidden advertisers. Some of these businesses do not advertise locally, but they are extremely proud of their community and are willing to support community events and promotions. They are great for signature pages and sponsorships.

Take the time to call on these businesses. There is not much competition. You see, no one is asking them to advertise.

Action Steps:

- Make a list of business you have not called on in the past
- Commit to making 1 to 2 calls on this group each week
- Your first call is just for fact finding and to introduce yourself
- Keep records on all the calls you complete
- Watch your sales increase

> "*The man on top of the mountain didn't fall there.*"
> —Anonymous

Prospecting—The Lifeblood of Sales

Prospecting is one of the easiest and the hardest aspects of selling. Where do you find additional customers? How does a sales person continue to increase sales and personal income year after year? What do successful sales people do? Here are some ways to prospect and find additional customers.

First of all, join a civic organization and become an active member. Join organizations like the Lions, Rotary, Optimists, JCs, or the local chamber of commerce. These groups have members that are community leaders, business owners, and managers. By volunteering your time and talents you will soon make friends with your fellow club members. These groups tend to be very close and support their fellow members. Not only will you gain new customers you will be doing something that is worthwhile for the community. Most civic organizations meet weekly and have special projects from time to time. The meetings are often at noon and last for an hour.

Secondly, successful sales people practice chain prospecting. This is the easiest way of all to get referrals. When you have established a solid working relationship with one of your customers, simply say something like,

"Mr. Jones, we have been working together on your advertising for several months. If you know of anyone else who could use my help, I would appreciate you giving them my name."

This works because you are not asking them to give you a list of people. Your customer most likely will not have any one in mind when you make the request, but from that time on your customer will be a walking testimonial for you to fellow business owners or managers in his area. It gets results because ad sales people always seem to be so busy that their customers have no idea that they are looking for additional customers to serve. It is a successful approach because people like to talk about their success and since you have been helping with his advertising you are one of your customer's successes.

Successful sales people also prospect by following up on sales leads. It is surprising how few businesses have a plan on how calls in sales inquiries are handled. Often there is an initial inquiry and then a media kit is mailed. That is it. The customer is supposed to read all the information in the media kit, become a media expert, sell themselves an ad, and call to place the order. Guess what? It will not happen.

To gain these potential customers go to your manager or publisher with a well thought-out plan on how you are going to handle call in customer inquiries. No one else is going to do it. The plan needs to show just how you will start at the beginning of the sales process and how you will track the steps of the sale and report on the progress. It is a lot of work but with the help of a computer it will not take a great amount of time and much can be done during slow-selling times. This is way above cold calling since these people called in because they were interested in your paper. They were so interested that they called to get additional information.

The last tip for prospecting is to "speak up." Tell people what you do. Let them know that you are an advertising sales person. The number one reason why people do not buy from a business or an individual is because the customer does not know what products or services a business or a sales person sells. Hand out business cards. In all my years of sales I have never heard of a manager or a publisher complaining that one of his or her sales people used too many business cards. Have them with you all the time. If someone needs to make a note, give him or her your card. They will carry it for several days or weeks. These are little billboards that say, "I help people with their advertising needs."

The real key to prospecting is to make sure to prospect all the time. To increase your sales, new prospects have to be added constantly. Prospecting is the lifeblood of successful sales people.

Action Steps:
- Join a civic organization in your community
- Practice chain prospecting
- Follow up on sales leads
- Tell people what you do and always have business cards with you
- Never stop prospecting

"In order to succeed, at times you have to make something from nothing."
—Ruth Mickleby-Land

Saving the Store

In my hometown we have the most wonderful hardware store in the world. It has isle after isle of tools, house wares, and supplies. Mike O'Hara, my best friend in high school, happened to be the son of the owner. The 2 of us spent many evenings and weekends stocking shelves, building displays, and listening to the stories that Mike's father would tell. One of his favorite stories seems most fitting even today.

The worst time to open a hardware store was a year before the start of the Great Depression. Mr. O'Hara did just that. Of course he had no way of knowing what was about to happen. The Depression came and his business dried up to just a few customers a day, buying just what was absolutely necessary to get by. Things got worse and worse. The very life of the business was in peril. Mr. O'Hara always explained that he did not know enough to know that the hardware store could not make it. So, he just kept going. But, he always maintained that one single idea saved the store.

He knew that people would have to heat their homes during the cold Midwest winters. Many people depended on coal and wood-fired heating stoves. These heavy iron stoves were used in most kitchens and living rooms at the time. Family members would come in from the cold and huddle around the stove to get warm. Mr. O'Hara decided that he would become the best place in town where people would go when they needed a new stove.

The plan to become that place was quite unique. First, he only had 3 stoves in stock, but could get a replacement in a day or so from the wholesaler if he sold one. The first step of the plan called for having the service man, Charlie, set up a heating stove in the front window. After 2 days he had Charlie take the stove apart and load it in the truck at about 10 o'clock in the morning. There was Charlie working in the main display window for all to see. After the stove was loaded the truck left and came back an hour or so later and Charlie would unload the same stove at the back loading dock. Then one of the other stoves was set up and displayed in the front window.

A day or so later, Charlie would dismantle the second stove in the front window for all to see and load it in the truck. After an hour or so the truck was at the rear loading dock and the stove was unloaded. The third stove was then assembled in the display in the front window. This went on for weeks and weeks finally someone came in and bought the stove in the front window and Charlie delivered it for real.

So many heating stoves were being loaded from the display window that people started to think O'Hara Hardware was the best place to buy stoves. Everyone assumed that they must be the best place to get a heating stove because they sold so many. Charlie finally stopped making fake deliveries because he was making so many real deliveries. Mike is the owner of O'Hara Hardware now and we still talk about this story and how Mike's father saved the store.

What does this have to do with community papers? Quite a lot, really. People like to deal with businesses and people who are successful. They will place ads in your paper if they believe you are the best place to advertise. There are several ways to become known as the best. Testimonials letters from current advertisers is one way. Having a respectable number of classified ads is another. Being known as the paper to read when shopping for autos, groceries, real estate, home furnishing, or home improvement will tell advertisers that this is the best place to advertise. Your paper needs to build on its strengths and keep adding and expanding segments of advertisers like autos. Your audit is another important tool to show how your paper is the best. The readership study tells exactly what your readers plan to spend in the next 12 months on a number of goods and services. Brain storm about how the people at your paper can save the store. Remember, perception often becomes reality.

Action Steps:

- As a team, pick a segment you want to see increased advertising
- List all the positives about your paper
- Develop a plan that allows you to succeed in attracting this group
- Once you have one group advertising go after another group
- Be sure to use your audit and readership studies when talking to each group

> *"Before everything else, getting ready is the secret of success"*
> —Henry Ford

Selling Success

There are as many different ways to sell as there are people trying to sell. No one has the corner on the right way to go about the process. I have read my share of books on selling and constantly buy more to read about the subject. In all of those books there seems to be a few reoccurring themes.

1. <u>Know your product.</u> This sounds so easy, until you start to realize that it means you also have to know your paper and how it compares to all the other media in the market. You have to know how your paper will help your customers.
2. <u>Know your customer.</u> This means that you have to be able to see your customers' business from their perspective. What are they trying to accomplish with their advertising? Too often we assume it is increased sales. What objective are they trying to achieve? Is it to inform, educate, attract new customer, reward existing customer, improve their image, or create a new image? What are their needs? Your customers are not concerned that you need to make a sale.

3. <u>Be prepared.</u> There are no salespeople who last in the selling of print advertising that just "wing it". There are some order takers but they never actually sell an ad. Being prepared means that you are offering your customer solutions to fill their needs. It means that you are organized. It means you have goals.
4. <u>Have integrity.</u> This means so many different things to people but it boils down to doing what you say you will do, being honest, admitting to mistakes and not over promising. When you have established integrity, then you are working with your customer to place advertising that solves their need.

Years ago, one of my sales reps was calling on the largest grocery chain in our market. They had 4 stores and invested thousands of dollars each week for advertising. My rep had made several calls on them to gather information. He put together a proposal and asked me to go with him to make the call. The 4 managers had a meeting every Friday morning and we had 15 minutes of their time. We arrived 5 minutes early and they were informed we were there. Thirty minutes later one of the managers came out and invited us in. We gave our proposal, they all seemed to agree and they told us they would let us know.

Two and half weeks went by and we had heard nothing. We got another meeting arranged and we again had to cool our heels for a while before we were invited in. We started in discussing the proposal that was given 3 weeks ago and one of the managers said that they already knew about that and were we here to waste more of their time? We both felt sick to the stomach. Out of somewhere I said. "No. Last time we told you about us. We are here to find out what you need and how we can help make your job easier. What problems do you have now?"

They started unloading every bad experience that they had from the paper they were presently using. One manager would actually spend 8 hours doing a complete layout of their double truck ad each week and give it to the other paper's rep because there had been too many mistakes in the past. What they wanted was their own 8-page tab on canary paper with black and red ink. They wanted a printing and insertion price that was good for the year. They wanted us to also print 20,000 additional copies to be inserted in to other papers. They wanted to have someone call on them that understood their business and have one person who would do the composition for them each week. They wanted to be able to proof the ad before it went to press.

We left with an appointment to meet the next Friday. We arrived early for the appointment and they greeted us and set aside the business they had been discussing. We gave them our proposal and outlined our answer to each concern. The sales rep had 6 years experience in the grocery business. We appointed one person to do the composition for their ad. We set up a time schedule that allowed for last minute changes and proofing of the ad at their Friday morning meeting. We secured a press time that allowed them to select sale items much closer to the distribution date of their insert. We added a few extras to make the transition as smooth as possible. They said yes and we picked up the largest account in town.

This all happened because we were given a second chance. A second chance to know our product, know our customer, be prepared, and have integrity. Just think how many other opportunities may have been lost because we did not get a second chance to do it the right way.

> **Action Steps:**
> - Prepare for each call
> - Do a needs analysis
> - Ask open-ended questions
> - Be a problem solver
> - Do it right the first time

"Unless you try to do something beyond what you have already mastered, you will never grow."
—Ronald E. Osborn

Short Course about Radio

Do you ever run up against an advertiser who uses radio and you would like to be able to have them send some of those dollars you way? The best way to understand how to sell against radio is to first understand why advertisers buy it. There are several positive aspects about radio advertising. They are:

1. They allow the advertiser to be target selective. Because different radio stations have different formats it is easy to select one that fits the audience the advertiser is trying to reach. If you want to reach the younger age group you select a station that plays their kind of music.
2. The advertiser can get a high frequency with an ad. The ad can be played over and over to the audience with the belief that the repetition will cause a call to action.
3. On a national or regional level the ad buy can be quite efficient in that there are networks of radio stations that can be purchased to help ease the placement of the commercials.
4. The radio is a portable and personal medium for many people. It is easy to carry a radio with you.

There is one in your car and often one playing in the background at work.
5. Radio can be used to transfer an image from a TV ad. In this way the advertiser is getting the impact of the TV ad, but for a lot less cost. This only works if there has been a significant amount of money spent on TV. For example, a radio ad that was the voice of the Maytag repairman bemoaning that he is the loneliest man in town, only works if the radio audience has that picture from the TV ad in their mind.
6. Radio can have a rather low production cost. All that is required is a script and a recording device. There is a person at the station who writes these scripts and the radio personalities record the commercial messages. It is easy to edit and change the ads and often at no additional cost.
7. Local personalities are often used in radio ads to add credibility to the message. While this person may be well known in the local community, they have no such importance regionally or nationally. Therefore, the cost for them to read a commercial is quite low.
8. Radio ads can also help when there are special merchandising opportunities. If a shipment of electric fans just arrived and your area is setting new records for high temperatures, with enough ads radio can help move the merchandise.

That is the list of why advertisers buy radio. Now take some time to look at the weaknesses of the media. There are several and any one can cause your advertiser to re-think the commitment to radio.

1. There are few restrictions when it comes to "commercial clutter". Have you ever noticed how

there is often one commercial after the other. Often there are 5 or more ads in a row. With all the ads there are fewer songs or news broadcast to entice the listener. The radio station is cluttered with ads and listeners tend to tune out the commercials or switch to another station.

2. Then too, some radio station formats are less involving to the listeners. The format may be compared to elevator music. You know it is on but you have no idea what is being played or said.
3. Each time the advertiser's ad is aired it is only heard by a relatively small audience. In order to get any kind of results the ad must be run frequently which in turn leads to commercial clutter. When the radio sales rep starts talking about a frequency schedule the low cost of one ad is now multiplied many times and for several days.
4. The audience of a radio station is often fractionalized which means the ad must run in various time slots in order to reach various people who may have an interest in the product or service the advertiser is trying to sell.
5. The cost to attain a significant reach can easily become quite high. The ad must run several times to the same audience in order to get results. To attract more than one segment of the listeners the ads must be run over and over to the new group of listeners.
6. Radio does not have a visual element so it is difficult to convey product identification or package recognition.
7. There are certain times of the day when the radio audience is at its greatest. Often, in order to get these positions the advertiser must also take times that have little or no value as far as advertising goes.

8. Often the best times are packaged and sold in advance to existing advertisers and it is difficult for a new advertiser to get the preferred time.
9. It is often difficult to get accurate data about smaller radio stations. It makes it extremely difficult for the advertiser to know what they are buying.
10. Compare the cost of a radio spot per thousand reach to readers per thousand to an ad in your paper and the cost for your paper will be less. In order to compare you need to get to a common denominator. A spot that costs $15.00 and reaches 50 people out of 1000 is extremely expensive on a per thousand basis. It is $300.00 per thousand. You can prove the reach of your ad with the audit and the cost is significantly less per thousand. A $300.00 ad in a paper with a circulation of 10,000 and a readership of 1.75 means 17,500 people are reading the paper or a cost of $17.14 per thousand.

The next time your customer starts talking radio, you will have some information about the competition. Only when you are aware of the strengths and the weaknesses can you handle a sales situation and come out on top.

Action Steps:

- Secure rate information about competing radio stations in your market
- Learn the strong and weak aspect of radio advertising
- Be prepared to show how your papers are a better value than radio
- Probe for dissatisfaction your customer has experienced with radio

"We are what we repeatedly do. Excellence, then, is not an act, but a habit."
—Aristotle

So What?

Two of the most important words to a sales person are—"So what?" Of all the things we can say, why those two words? A typical advertising sales person will say things like:

"We have a circulation of 25,000."
"We have the best graphic artist on our staff."
"We have been around since 1965."
"We carry all the major food stores."

What is the response to all of these statements? You guessed it—"So what?" Sales people are really good at listing all the features about their paper but they do not do so well in converting the feature into a benefit. If a sales person is calling on a hardware store and they see a lot of new lawn mowers, the conversation should go something like this:

"Mr. Jones, I see you have several new lawn mowers in your inventory. Do you know the XYZ paper goes to 25,000 homes each week? What this means to you is that every home in your market gets a copy of our paper and your ad will go to all of your customer and potential customers. Our paper reaches the very homes you need to reach. You know the ones that need a new lawn mower."

The sales person just took a dull statement about a circulation of 25,000 and answered the question—"So what?" The sales person turned the feature into a benefit that was relevant to the owner of the hardware store.

As sales people we feel comfortable talking about our papers and using terms that mean something to us. These same terms mean very little to your customer. A readership score on your audit of 78% means nothing to an advertiser. However, when you say that 98% of the homes in the market receive the paper and of those homes 78% read the paper. That means that 3 out of 4 homes in the market will be exposed to the customers advertising message. There is no other advertising medium that can come close to that type of coverage and market penetration.

Selling by the numbers is an expansion of answering—"So what?". Many papers have done readership studies to find out what the readers will be buying the next 12 months. To say that 21% of the homes we deliver to are going to buy a used or new car or truck in the next 12 months does not mean much to the auto dealer. But if your paper's circulation is 25,000 and 98% of the market say they receive it and 78% of the homes that receive it say they read it then, we now can really answer the question.

$$25{,}000 \times .98 = 24{,}500$$
$$24{,}500 \times .78 = 19{,}110$$

Of those 19,110 homes that read the paper 21% or 4,013 are going to buy a new or used car or truck in the next 12 months.

"Mr. Auto Dealer, would you agree that roughly 25% will be new cars? The National Auto Dealers Association estimates that the average price of a new car is $26,300. Would you agree that the average price of a used car is $9,000?" If he disagrees use the numbers he gives you. 1,003 (.25 × 4013) new cars will be purchased for over $26 million (1,003 × $26,300) and additionally over $27 million (.75 × 4,013 = 3,009 × $9,000) will be spent on used cars. "Mr. Auto Dealer, our readers are going to be spending over $53 million for autos and trucks. These are just the buyers that said they were going to buy. Should not your advertising be in the paper that can get your message to the people who are going to buy?"

I once went through a training exercise where we did role playing. Whenever the person representing the sales person would state a feature and not follow up with the benefit, the entire class would yell out—"So what?" Even today, that phrase is still with me whenever I make a sales call. Never talk about a feature of your paper without answering the question—"So what?" Remember you are only talking about your paper unless you are answering the question—"So what?" Once you do, you are selling.

Action Steps:

- Make a list of all the features about your paper
- Now turn that feature into a benefit
- Practice, Practice, and Practice some more
- Mentally ask "So what?" as you give your presentation
- Enjoy your selling success

"One of life's most painful moments comes when we must admit that we didn't do our homework, that we are not prepared."
—Merlin Olsen

Taking a Hard Look

I recently went on a sales call with a print advertising sale rep. We talked a lot about the sales call and what little he knew about the client. I thought this person would be totally prepared for the call. I was wrong. Maybe the fact that I was there contributed to his nervousness. However, I think it came from not being totally prepared.

Being the guest on the call is so much easier than making the call. However, there are certain things that the sales person must do before arriving at the customer's office. The first is to have an objective for making the call. It may be as simple as just trying to arrange an appointment. It maybe to gain facts about the customer's business or it could be to gain some insight into the customer's needs. No matter what the objective of the call is, once the objective is accomplished the call is a success. In this case there was not a clear cut objective so the call went in several directions.

The second mistake happened when the sales person realized that there would only be one person in the room instead of 4. He immediately went into fast mode and gave the impression that he just wanted to get through the call as soon as possible. You can imagine how the customer felt. Whether the call is given to one person or 20 people a true sales person will treat the call as the most important thing happening for the client at that point in time—because, it is.

The third mistake was not being completely prepared for the call. The PowerPoint presentation was used as a crutch and not as a sales tool. The sales person could have just as easily look at his computer screen and not turn and talk to the screen on the wall. Because the sales person was facing the customer and the screen was behind him, much of the time during the presentation he had his back to the client. On top of that, the presentation was rushed and thus disjointed.

The fourth mistake happened because the comments made during the presentation did not allow for client interaction. The sales person did not ask for agreement on any points or ask for customer input. There was no fact finding questions asked either close ended or open ended. The sales person just started talking and did not stop to ask questions. The only positive information came from the customer as an observation.

The fifth mistake was to not set a time to get back in touch with the client. Other than to say that some additional information would be sent there was no mention of a follow up call. This leaves the salesperson with very little reason to make the next call or for the customer to accept a call.

The sixth mistake was to see the call as potential business. We did not learn enough to know what to do next. The customer is most likely confused as to why we were there. If I had been the customer I would not believe that the sales person had done anything that wanted me to talk to him again. We may have had the answers to solve their needs but we did not find out what those needs were.

Where do we go from here? We step back and start building on the only information that was provided to us. A sales call that could have been so promising turned into one that will require so much more work on our part. We have only one small piece of information for a clue as to how we proceed. The sales cycle has just gotten longer for this account. We lost the momentum that was ours at the beginning of the sales call. I hope the customer did not become lost as well. I am confident we could have helped this customer and in time we may regain the opportunity.

Action Steps:

- Always be prepared for the call
- Do not assume you know what the customer needs
- Be sure to do fact finding
- Arrange for a call-back opportunity
- Be professional

> *"Kind words can be short and easy to speak, but their echoes are truly endless."*
> —Mother Teresa

The Success Secret

There is one secret that almost guarantees that you will be a success in your sales career. It does not take a large amount of time. You do not have to spend hours in a classroom or even listen to some so called super sales person talk about themselves. The cost is almost nothing. The secret is the practice of sending out 5 handwritten "Thank You" notes a week.

The message can be a short simple statement of how much you appreciate their business. You may want to thank them for sending a new customer your way. How about thanking them for helping out on some community committee? There never seems to be a shortage of reasons to thank someone, once you start thinking about it. And, there lies the problem. We do not think about thanking people, let alone taking the few extra minutes to do what needs to be done to make a difference.

There is someone out there who has done something for you that warrants a thank you. Are you going to let this opportunity slip by? If you are like the other sales people calling on your customer you will. Here is your chance to rise above everyone else because none of them are going to send a thank you note. Do you remember the last thank you note you received? It is a silly question because we all do. Sending a thank you note makes a positive impression.

Tim Connor, from the old Salesdoctors.com website, suggests:

1. Call at least one person a day to thank him or her for something.
2. Send out 5 thank you notes a week.
3. Do not wait to show your appreciation. Do it now.
4. Do what you do for others without the expectation of appreciation. When you want something back, that is not a gift—it is barter.
5. Send a special friend a surprise gift. (It does not have to be expensive; it is really the thought that counts.)

There is nothing for you to lose. It does not cost you anything to say "thank you." Yet, it means so much to the people and the customers who have helped you. Here is you opportunity to succeed. Practice this program for 1 month and it will become a habit. Each thank you is a seed planted and in the end the harvest is all yours.

> **Action Steps:**
> - Buy some blank Thank You note cards
> - Commit to sending out 5 thank you cards a week
> - Do this for a month
> - Enjoy how good you feel about yourself

> "Failure is the opportunity to begin again more intelligently"
> —Henry Ford

The Top Ten (plus 5) Reasons Print Advertising Sales People Fail

I started asking print advertising sales people why they think other sales people in the same position do not succeed. The answers came fast a furious. Maybe you will see one or two of these problems that you have as a sales person. If so, now is a good time to take corrective action.

1. **They do not work.** They put in the time but they are working on non-productive activities. Such as building a client database on the computer. They have all sorts of data on the customer, but they do not make the calls.
2. **They over promise and under deliver.** When making the sale they will promise to do any number of things for the client and after the sale is made forget all about those promises. Unfortunately, the customer does not forget.
3. **They do not have established personal sales goals.** The sales people have not established realistic sales goals and become frustrated because they are not making more money or they are constantly under pressure to achieve certain sales levels. Because,

the goals are not their goals the likelihood of achieving them is greatly diminished.

4. **They do not have a plan on how to achieve their goals.** Failure to plan is planning to fail. Nothing is accomplished until there is some sort of a plan. The sales people who plan their days and weeks are the ones who succeed. They constantly monitor their results so they can adjust their plan.
5. **They spend too much time trying to land one big account.** It is easy to get caught in the belief that if only XYZ Mega Mart would start advertising with me everything would be great. The problem evolves because the sales person is spending too much time on this one potential account and neglects all of the smaller accounts that can keep the sale pipeline full. It is OK to hunt the elephants as long as you hunt a few rabbits along the way so you can eat.
6. **They do not take care of existing customers.** The sales person feels that the accounts have been running in the paper regularly and they put them in an automatic mode. Sooner or later the neglected customer will give the business to some one who will give them some TLC.
7. **They do not prepare for sales calls.** The sales people start believing that they are so good as a sales person that they can just wing a presentation. After awhile they stop preparing for any calls and their closing rate drops way off. They continue to make sales calls to fewer and fewer customers.
8. **They do not seek training in sales.** The sales people feel that they already know how to sell so why bother with more training. They often say that they have heard it all before and nothing new comes out

of training. They fail to realize that even seasoned sales people need to be trained and retrained. The constant training keeps the sales people sharp and in tune with their clients.

9. **They do not make cold calls.** Some sales people feel that it is beneath them to solicit new customers. Others may have developed cold call reluctance and are afraid of rejection because they have allowed the rejection to become personal. Whatever the reason, making cold calls keeps the sales pipeline full.

10. **They think too much about themselves.** Instead of doing what is best for the customer they do what is best for them. Rather than build a long-lasting relationship they try to squeeze the maximum amount of sales from the customer as soon as possible. The sales person gets more up front that way but loses it all in the end.

11. **They do not handle problems well.** Rather than address the problem and getting past it, they hope that it will just go away. In the end they have to face the issue. It never just goes away.

12. **They waste a lot of time.** Since the sales people do not have a plan they are faced with times when they feel there is nothing to do. This is often the time they become engrossed in non-productive busy work.

13. **They gossip about other customers.** The salesperson will gossip about another customer to a customer. While the customers the sales person is speaking to may enjoy the story, in the back of their mind they are wondering what the sales person is saying about them. This leads to a breakdown in trust and lost sales.

14. **They do not return phone calls.** Many sales people tend to be lazy about returning phone calls. They may be avoiding a disgruntled client or they may prejudge the person's reason for calling. By not returning phone calls they are showing disrespect to that person. Besides not getting all the sales that they could, they also start losing customers who move on to someone that will return calls and take care of them.
15. **They do not listen.** There is an old saying in sales. It goes like this, "You have two ears and one mouth. Use them in that proportion." Sales people tend to want to do all of the talking. The sale comes from listening to the customer.

By understanding some of the problems that print advertising sales people have, you can either change a habit or catch yourself before one of these problems becomes a routine. Your success is based on several factors, recognizing that you may be falling into one of these traps is the first step.

Action Steps:

- Keep this list handy
- Review it often to recognize a potential problem
- Take corrective action immediately
- Continue to review the list regularly

> *"Feeling gratitude and not expressing it is like wrapping a present and not giving it."*
> —William Arthur Ward

There Is No "I" in TEAM

A while back, my wife was in charge of coordinating an office move for her department at the University of Iowa. One day she was telling me about how some of the people were acting just like children because they did not get a window or that the individual offices were smaller than a few of the old ones. She asked me what I would say to these people when they came complaining. I told her to tell them that "There Is No I in TEAM." After all, the move was to better space that is being remodeled especially for them.

In sales we often believe that we are the only ones generating revenue. Sales people tend to believe and feel that they work alone. Most of the time, they do not have another person with them when they perform their job. Consequently, much of the day is spent with little contact with fellow employees. Under these circumstances it is easy to get into the "I" way of thinking. Such as: I did this or that. I made the sale. I generated the revenue.

But, "There is No I in TEAM." Stop and think of all the people who make what you sell possible. Just in your office there are numerous people supporting you. They include your publisher, manager, editors, reporters, composition people, front office staff, prepress people, pressman, truck drivers, and delivery people. Then there are the customers and the readers of your paper.

It is truly a team effort. Should any one of these people fail to do their job to support you, the ad you sold is not what you promised the customer. You have to rely on these people or you have nothing to sell. Imagine trying to sell a paper that claimed 30,000 in circulation and the delivery people only distributed 20,000. It would not take long for your customers to realize that your paper did not give them the ROI they expected.

When was the last time you told the people who help you day in and day out how much you appreciate their effort and work? Have you ever gone to the person that composed the ad and told them that the customer was really happy with the ad? How about the front office staff, they can make you look good to a customer by how they sound on the phone or how they act when a customer walks in. Most people want to do a good job and the number one motivator is appreciation.

Today ad sales are so competitive and the advertising opportunities for your customer seem to be almost endless. As a sales person you need all the support you can get to keep your customers happy. According to recent research, 75% of satisfied or very satisfied customers will leave you for a better deal. The days of old fashion customer loyalty are gone. Consumers are constantly seeking out the best deal. You and your paper are not isolated from this either.

Businesses still buy from the sales person that takes care of them and offers honest value for the advertising space they need. This can only happen consistently if the sales person is a team player. It takes a team to serve your customer. You cannot do it by yourself. Just remember that TEAM stands for—Together Everyone Achieves More.

Action Steps:

- Become a TEAM player
- Show appreciation to TEAM members
- Give credit to members of your TEAM
- Let your customers know that there is a TEAM working behind the scenes

> "To become successful you must be a person of action. Merely to "know" is not sufficient. It is necessary both to know and do."
>
> —Napoleon Hill

Truly Amazing

I want to tell you about a couple of things that happened recently that are truly amazing.

First of all, I am a firm believer in the power of "Thank you notes, letters, or cards." They work because we all like to be thanked. Right now you can remember a "thank you" you have received. There is no other tool a sales person has that can come close to the power of a thank you note. I am talking about written personal thank you notes not e-mails. They take just a few minutes to write and have a lasting impact.

I am on a board that is involved with mentally and physically challenged children. We are constantly raising money for this organization. One of the things this organization does is send each and every person who makes a contribution a thank you letter that is personalized by the director. Many people support this organization and when they pass away their families request memorials to be sent to the organization. About 10 years ago a lady from out of state sent a check for $25.00 because of just such a request by a family. She received a thank you letter that explained how her donation would be used to help the children. We never heard from her again, but we kept her name in the computer database as a contributor.

Now, 10 years later we got a call from an attorney stating that the organization had been remembered in some lady's will. The database was checked and the record of the $25.00 donation was found along with a notation that a thank you letter had been sent. That was the only contact we ever had with this person. Now, she was leaving something to the organization in her will. How powerful can a thank you letter be? Well, just last week we received a check from the lady's estate for $500,000.00. That is correct. One thank you letter was worth a half a million dollars to this lady.

The second amazing thing happened a few weeks ago. I was fortunate enough to be invited to a concert in a major metro area by a friend who is a VP for a large newspaper. His paper has a skybox where the event was held and he had a couple of tickets that were given back at the last minute. So my wife and I accepted his offer.

The skybox is used to reward clients and entice prospective clients to do business with the paper. He was the only representative there from the paper and was the host for the evening. We had plenty of things to eat and drink. My friend treated the 15 guests as if they were VIPs. He knew who was attending, and greeted everyone. There was no high pressure selling going on. But, it was obvious to me, as an observer, that our host was well prepared. He knew sales information about each account that was attending. He also knew something about the current situation with each account.

Before the concert started, our host was talking to 2 men and their wives when the men brought up something about advertising. They were saying how expensive it had become and how they would like to get more impact for their dollar. Our host immediately replied that he thought he could show them a way to increase their lineage and not spend any more than they currently were on print. He told them that his best guess was that they were spending about $800,000.00 a year in newspaper advertising—when you added up all of the different businesses they owned. The customers agreed. It was pointed out to them that if they would consolidate their print advertising contracts into one, then they would be at a much lower contract rate. Thus, by consolidating all the contracts for the various businesses and by placing their print buy in to one paper they would get so much more for the same amount of money.

Our host then said, "The concert is about ready to start. Let me take you to lunch next week and we can discuss it more. If you need to bring others in on invite them too. Please, enjoy the concert with your wives."

After the concert the men thanked our host, said they had a wonderful time, and they were anxious about the meeting next week. One of the men added there would not be any problem and thanked him for inviting them and helping them out.

Being prepared and taking the time to learn something about the account allowed my friend to land the sale. It was amazing to see a true advertising professional at work. I asked him how much more his paper would get from the new arrangement. His response was that the dollars spent by the customer would double for his paper. He just brought in another $400,000.00.

Remember to thank people and be prepared. It pays off.

Action Steps:
- Continue to write thank you notes
- Always be prepared for a sales situation
- Work to improve your skills as a sales person

> "The weak can never forgive. Forgiveness is the attribute of the strong"
> —Gandhi

Use a Big Eraser

As a sales person your attitude about yourself and others is constantly on display for all to see. People can sense when you are happy and when you are not. The way you feel about yourself and others has a major impact on how well you do your job. In sales a proper attitude is critical. One of the best ways to become happy is to learn to forgive other people.

I once went through a legal dispute where someone had sued me. Although I won the case, for over a year I would not let myself be in a face-to-face situation with that person. One day it occurred to me that I was being controlled by the other person. I was allowing this to happen. I was the one making the changes in my life. Shortly thereafter, I saw the person in a restaurant. I worked up all my courage, walked over to the table and told that person that I knew we had our disagreements in the past but that I only wished him and his family the very best. From that day on, we spoke to each other whenever we met. The negative feelings left and my attitude improved over night.

Wayne Dwyer author of the book titled <u>Pulling Your Own Strings</u> talks about how other people have control of your actions. Have you ever crossed to the other side of the street so you would not have to come face to face with someone? Because of deep hurt and anger you did not want to face that person. It is a common experience for all of us. As Dwyer points out, that person is controlling your actions. Whether you want to admit it or not that person caused you to do something.

Another time, during the process of selling a business I was collecting the outstanding accounts receivable. The figure was down to less than a half of a percent of the total. No matter how hard I tried I could not get these last few people to pay what they owed. This bothered me to no end until I realized that there was not a very good chance of ever being paid. The next week I went to every one of those customers and told them that I thought that they were a decent person and if they had the money they would pay me what they owed. But, I was going to forgive the debt and they owed me nothing. I did not feel that I was owed money by any of these people and I felt great. They felt great and over the years some of those people actually paid me.

It all happened because of a change in my attitude and learning the power of forgiveness. I decided that I was not going to carry all that excess baggage. I did not want those negative feelings controlling my life. I did not want to show up at a customer's office preoccupied with destructive feelings. I wanted to have a peaceful attitude about my life and forgiving others allowed that to happen.

This is an attitude change that you can start doing right now. You do not have to spend any money. You have everything to gain and nothing to lose. Will you get hurt again? Yes. Will it be from some of the same people? Most likely. That is the only downside to forgiveness. Imagine how relieved you are going to feel when you leave all the old unwanted baggage behind. And you can mend a friendship, salvage a customer, strengthen a relationship or encourage a co-worker. Watch your sales grow as you become more relaxed and not so uptight.

In all of our religious teachings, no matter what religion you follow, forgiveness is a basic principle. Christianity certainly teaches forgiveness, Author Billy Zeoli sums it up when he states "God has a big eraser".

Action Steps:

- Take control of your attitude
- Remember—Is your attitude worth catching
- Learn to forgive others
- Enjoy the new you

> *"Promise only what you can deliver. Then deliver more than you promise."*
>
> —Author Unknown

We Promise

My wife and I recently stayed at a Fairfield Inn & Suites by Marriott. When we walked in the door we were treated with respect and made to feel welcome. Everything about our stay was pleasant and the hotel staff was so nice and accommodating. I did not spend a great amount of time thinking about it, but decided that if we were to return to this city we would stay at that same hotel again.

On the desk in the room was a card that stated that at Fairfield Inn & Suites by Marriott, a promise made is a promise kept. The card went on...

> "You're our guest, and guests are our highest priority at Fairfield Inn/Fairfield Inn & Suites. So much so, that each of us has made you a promise, signed it, and displayed it in our lobby as a reminder of your importance... and our commitment.

We Promise to:

- Always make you feel welcome
- Always give you a room that's clean, fresh, and reflects the highest quality standards

- Always respond promptly to any need you may have
- Always give you the service that will make you want to return

If for any reason, you believe we're not keeping our word, please tell us immediately. After all, a promise is a promise."

What would be the impact if each member of your staff made such a promise? Could or would all of your staff be able to honestly sign such a promise. Just suppose that everyone at your paper signed such a promise and it was displayed in the front office. Would the quality of work increase? Would better ads be produced? Would the distribution of the paper improve? Would there be fewer problems between departments? Would sales go up? Would the paper be a fun place to work? Would people start to notice the difference? The answer to all of these questions is "yes".

> "You're our advertiser, and advertisers are our highest priority at (Your paper's name). So much so, that each of us has made you a promise, signed it, and displayed it in our front office as a reminder of your importance . . . and our commitment.

We Promise to:

- Always make you feel welcome and appreciated
- Always give you our best work that reflects the highest quality standards
- Always respond promptly to any need you may have
- Always give you the service that will make you want to continue doing business with us

If for any reason, you believe we're not keeping our word, please tell us immediately. After all, at (Your paper's name) a promise is a promise."

The promise clearly explains to the staff that the customer is extremely valuable and allows them to take pride an ownership in doing their best. We all need gentle reminders to keep us focused on what is truly important in our jobs. Making and keeping a promise to customers is the cornerstone of all successful businesses because "a promise made is a promise kept".

Action Steps:

- Make a poster with the appropriate wording
- Have everyone sign it (This can be used for a team, department, or entire company.)
- Display the poster in a prominent place
- Remind everyone about their promise

"Good advertising does not just circulate information. It penetrates the public mind with desires and belief."
—Leo Burnett

What Advertising Can Do

Many advertisers and print advertising sales people are confused about what advertising can do. Each week, advertising is placed in publications and often the expectations of the advertiser are not reached. If there is a clear understanding of what the ad is designed to do, evaluating the success of the ad, or ad campaign, becomes easier. Below is a list on what advertising can do.

1. **Provide Information.** This may be about store hours and location or information about products and services offered. Advertising can successfully be used to inform client and potential clients about almost anything.
2. **Create Desire.** Advertising can be used to build up desire for goods and services. How many people use cell phones today? Ten years ago, the number was quite small. Advertising created the desire and today almost everyone has a cell phone.
3. **Narrow Down Choices for Buyers.** Everyday we are bombarded with thousands of advertising messages. Proper advertising can help in narrowing

the selection process. It may be done with price, product features and benefits, or availability.
4. **Lower the Selling Cost per Customer.** Well planned and thought out advertising can actually lower the selling cost for the business. Think of a business that needs to generate leads for their sales people, as more leads are generated, more sales calls are made, more sales are closed, and the cost per sale goes down.
5. **Blanket Prospects with a Message.** The ad can let everyone know something about the business or products that are offered. A furniture store may be adding a new line of recliners. They can let the prospects in their market know that the store now carries the new brand.
6. **Influence People to Feel a Need for Products or Services.** By designing an ad in the correct way, people are persuaded to feel a need for a particular product or service. An ad, or ad campaign, that lists what to look for when it is time to replace the roof on a house can create a need for a roofing company. Since a specific roofing company ran the ad, that company will increase the number of calls they get.
7. **Regulate Traffic Flow.** Most retail and service businesses do not have a constant flow of people in and out of their place of business. By advertising specials and offering incentives during particular times a business can level out the flow of traffic and often increase its total number of customers. Think of a movie theater. Not many people go in the middle afternoon. However, with the matinee discount not only are new customers being attracted to the

theater, the cost of showing the film one more time is almost nothing.
8. **Encourage Consumers to Ask for More Information.** Some items require the consumer to seek more information before making a buying decision. A well-done ad can encourage those people to ask at a particular business as opposed to its competition.
9. **Favorably Position a Business In the Consumer's Mind.** Advertising can be used to build upon the good reputation of a business. If the business has been in the community for several years, it is important to let people know. Published testimonials will help promote a good impression. It is building a brand for a particular business.
10. **Contribute to the Success of the Business.** F. D. Van Amburgh said it best, "Intelligent, effective advertising is not an expense—it is insurance against the loss of business that the other fellow is fighting for."
11. **Influence Future Sales.** Many businesses that sell large ticket items must advertise not for today but for the sales that will happen in the future. A real estate companies and auto dealers are prime examples. By advertising, they are able to keep their name in front of the buyer when the buyer is ready to make a purchase.
12. **Create a Sense of Urgency.** Advertising can drive traffic to a business right now. This is done all the time by running a special promotion or special pricing that has a limited number of days. Food store use this all the time. They have specials that draw customers into the store.
13. **Allow Business to Compete.** The best way to compete with another like business is to advertise.

Advertising is the only effective way to get the message to potential customers and drive traffic to the business.

14. **Keep a Business Alive.** The business that stops advertising to save money is like the man who stops the clock to save time.

You can increase your sales and the success of your clients' advertising if you explain to them what their ad is designed to accomplish. If the client wants to create immediate traffic and sales and your ad is designed to increase future sales, neither one of you will be happy with the results. By understanding what advertising can do both of you will be working with the same goal in mind.

Action Steps:

- Ask your customers what they want their ad to do
- Be sure you both understand the reason behind the ad
- Keep this list for reference

"Every great business is built on friendship."
—J.C. Penney

What Happened

A while ago, an old junior high school classmate sent me an email. I was totally taken off guard. This person was someone who had been a good friend in eighth grade but we just drifted apart in high school and have not seen each other since graduation. Customers, like friends sometimes just drift away.

We can all remember a customer who ran consistently with the paper week in and week out. Then the ads sort of dropped off and now they do not advertise in the paper at all. These great former customers are just lost in the routine of day-to-day business. Maybe their sales rep left and no one serviced their account any more. Maybe a mistake or a situation was never resolved. Maybe they were not treated as a valuable customer. There are many reasons for the loss of the advertiser. The important thing is what are you doing to win that customer back?

When I heard from my old friend, my thoughts did not go to any negative aspect of the friendship. Only positive thoughts came to mind. Most likely your lost customer has many positive thoughts about your paper. The first step in winning the customer back is to contact the customer. Next, arrange to meet the customer in person and just get to know them. You should spend 90% of this time talking about them and their needs and problems. Personally, I would not try to sell them an ad at this point but would leave the door open to come back with ideas that may help solve a problem or need.

After your meeting, write a thank you note to the lost customer for taking the time to visit with you. No one else is sending them a thank you note and the lost customer will remember. Just to show how powerful a thank you note is, right now you can remember the last thank you card you received. Everyone remembers being thanked in writing. You want this customer to remember you.

If the customer left because of some old unresolved issues, go to your manager and tell them about your conversation with the lost account. Many times the issue can be resolved on the spot. Often a customer will have a complaint or an issue about your paper and never tell the sales rep or anyone at the paper. They just take their business elsewhere. If the issue is somewhat more difficult to resolve, it would be appropriate to get your manager involved. In the end the goal is to get the issue resolved to everyone's satisfaction.

It is often said that people do not buy your product because of the product they buy because of the relationship they have with the sales person. This is also true at your paper. Customers become quite attached to "their sales rep." When that person is no longer with the paper they feel lost and left out. After all, their old rep always took care of them. If you are assigned such an account you need to start building a relationship as soon as possible. When there is a change in sales people that is the best time to start saving those accounts. Extra effort needs to be focused on them.

A lost customer is often easier to win than a new customer. After all, they know about your paper. Many times, you do not have to sell them on the merits of your paper. They used it successfully in the past. They may want to start out slowly and build back to the previous level of business. That is a great way to win them back. You may even want to suggest that they do that.

Customers are your livelihood. They decide the fate of your future. They are all worth saving.

> **Action Steps:**
> - Search for lost customers
> - Make appointments and call on these lost customers
> - Ask open-ended questions and listen to the answers
> - After the appointment send a Thank You card
> - Keep building the relationship

"To get what we've never had, we must do what we've never done."
—Anonymous

What have We Lost?

Over the past 50 years the community paper industry has lost millions of dollars in advertising. When everyone is scrambling for additional sales, money is left on the table on a regular basis. How does this happen? Listen in on an all too typical call to a community paper office.

A call from a regional or national media buyer goes something like this:

> *Media Buyer:* "Hello, I am Mary Media Buyer; I need to speak to someone about placing display advertising in your paper."
>
> *Paper's Receptionist:* "You will have to talk to Mr. Publisher. He is not in at the present time. Would you like his voice mail?"
>
> *Media Buyer:* "Will he be back soon or is there someone else who can help me?"
>
> *Paper's Receptionist:* "I am not sure when he will get back. He is the person to talk to. Would you like his voice mail?"
>
> *Media Buyer:* "Maybe you can help me. Do you know what your open rate is and the paper's circulation?"

Paper's Receptionist: "No, I am sorry." Would you like Mr. Publisher's voice mail?

Media Buyer: "I guess so." (to the voice mail message system) "Mr. Publisher, I am Mary Media Buyer and I have a client who is interested in running in your paper. I am on a tight deadline for information. Will you please call me by the end of the day? My number is 123-555-1234."

The paper has the ad by just making a phone call. What actually happens is that the call in many cases is not returned or is returned a couple of days too late. The next time Mary Media Buyer has client that wants Mr. Publisher's paper she will not even bother making the call and just give the ad to the other publication. I can tell you from experience that this happens too many times. When calling community papers, too often, we do not get the calls returned.

I even had buyers tell me that their client had asked for a specific community paper and they could not get the information so the print buy went to another publication. They went on to say that the community papers are sometimes the only way to reach the people and how wished the industry was doing something about it. Having a number to call and getting information would be a real plus.

Why not prepare a simple cheat sheet that lists the publications open rate, circulation, ad deadline, email address to receive ads, process color charges, insert rates, shipping address, and anything else that a media buyer might ask? Then give it to the receptionist to use when media buyers call and no one is there to answer the questions. Better yet, have the composition department design a one-page fact sheet with the above information that can be faxed to the media buyer. Be sure to have a space for the media buyer's name, company, telephone, and fax number. That way, the receptionist completes the information, faxes the form, and forwards the sheet to the appropriate person, at the paper, for follow up and action. This one sheet of paper would be handy for the outside sales reps as well.

Remember that over the past several years your publication has lost thousands of dollars because the interested media buyer could not get the information.

Action Steps:

- Design the one-page sheet described in the article
- Make sure everyone that has customer contact gets a proof copy
- Make any changes and corrections that are needed
- Have the composing people make an attractive info sheet
- Make enough copies so everyone with customer contact gets one
- Update whenever something on the sheet changes

> *"The will to win is not nearly as important as will to prepare to win."*
> —Bobby Knight

What is the Objective?

For many sales people a sales call that does not get a sale is a failure. These sales people lead an extremely frustrating life. We all know that each sales call is not going to result in a sale. There are sales people who have jobs that require a tremendous number of "no's" in order to make a sale. These people must have no fear of rejection and be able to see each "no" as a way to get closer to a "yes." They go through cold call after cold call each day and have the resilience to bounce back the next day. These sales people need an unlimited number of people to call. There are successful sales people who can do just that. They can get on the telephone and make call after call after call.

When I got out of college I wanted to be a stock broker. In order to be successful I needed to start out by making 100 cold calls a day. Out of those 100 calls 4 to 6 would actually want to talk to me. Over time, the statistics showed that of those 100 cold calls one person would do business with me sometime in the future. It was truly a numbers game. The burn out rate for new brokers was quite high. To get a feel for how this works, stand in front of a mirror and say "no" out loud to yourself 96 times. I lasted 3 years and jumped at the chance to go into business with one of my clients.

For most sales people there is not an unlimited supply of contacts. If you are assigned a territory your number of clients and potential clients is limited. In order to be successful in your territory you will have to call on the same clients on a fairly regular basis. How do you keep a positive attitude when working your territory? One of the best ways to do that is to establish objectives for each call. That way the call is a success if you are able to meet the objective. On a cold call may be your objective is to introduce yourself and your paper to a new business and start building a report. When you accomplish that task the call was a success. Should you happen to make a sale in the process—Great!

Each week when you plan for the next week think about what you want to accomplish on each call. Maybe you want to talk to a client about a special section that is coming up, maybe you want to explain the paper's latest audit information, or you will be asking for the order. How about setting up an appointment to help your customers prepare an advertising budget or to close on an advertising proposal you made earlier? There are obviously many other objectives that you can set. The important part is that when you meet the objective your call is a success.

If you embrace this attitude and set objectives for your calls, you start to feel better about yourself. When you feel better about yourself other people notice, people like family, friends, and business associates. Having an attitude that is based on success makes working with you a much more pleasant experience. That is why people like dealing with successful people.

Success is not accumulating an enormous amount of wealth or obtaining your ultimate goal. Success is a day-to-day activity and should be celebrated every step of the way. By setting objectives you will be able to enjoy the journey.

Action Steps:
- As you plan your calls for the next week list the objective for each call
- When you accomplish the objective mark the call as successful
- Be prepared to ask for the order—closing can happen anytime during a call
- Keep track of your daily successful calls

> *"The way to get started is to quit talking and begin doing."*
>
> —Walt Disney

What Successful Sales People Do

Over the past several years I have been asking successful advertising sales people why they are a success. The answers are extremely interesting and in some case a little surprising. Here are my top 10 responses:

1. **"At the end of the day when I feel that I am done, I make one more sales call."** What a great way to add an additional prospect call or follow up call. During a year that amounts to 236 additional calls.
2. **"I do not stop for lunch until I have 2 consecutive incidents where the decision maker is out to lunch."** Many sales people believe that small business owners are not around over the noon hour. They are wrong because in a lot of businesses the boss stays and works while his employees go to lunch at noon.
3. **"Every day I mail out a thank you card to someone. It may be a client, a business associate, or a community leader."** Most sales people do not even think about the power of sending out thank you cards. It takes so little time and the rewards are enormous.

4. **"I deliver my own tear sheets each week."** This gives you one more reason to be in front of the client. It shows that you are proud of the work you produce and assures the client that you are part of his team.
5. **"I plan my week on Friday afternoon for the next week."** The idea of planning your week in advance allows the sales person to be in control of their time. It assures that there is no wasted effort and maximizes the sales effort.
6. **"At the beginning of each year I sit down and set goals and develop a plan to achieve my goals."** We all know how important goal setting is but very few people actually do much about it. Investing 4 to 6 hours in setting goals and writing a plan on how to achieve those goals adds thousands of dollars to your pay each year.
7. **"Staying educated about my profession and my customers adds to my success."** As fast as everything is changing today a successful sales person has to be learning all the time. The way we did business 2 years ago is not the same as it is today. The only way to be successful is to invest in yourself.
8. **"I keep impeccable records on my clients. I know what they did last year and the year before that. I know when they typically have major sales."** Having this type of information can only help. It shows that the sales person cares and is planning and working for the customer. Being organized means that there is not a lot of wasted energy and time.
9. **"I find asking for referrals to be a key success factor for me."** Referrals are a sure way to get additional business. Most satisfied customers are happy to do this for you. If you do not ask, you will not get many referrals.

10. **"An answer of "No" does not mean that they are rejecting me. I just assume, at the time, they are not interested in the opportunity I am offering. I just continue calling on them."** This may seem like a small matter, but most sales people will stop calling on a customer after 2 visits and 2 "no's." Only 3% of sales people will go back 5 or more times. The average customer will say "no" 4 times before saying "yes".

If you decide to use one of these ideas, your sales will increase substantially. When you practice one of these procedures for a month it becomes a habit. When the action is a habit choose another and do it for a month. Now you have 2 habits that will ensure your success. In the end, you are the only person who can determine your success.

Action Steps:

- Select one of the ideas and use it for 30 days
- After 30 days you have formed a new habit
- Select another idea and use it for 30 days
- You now have 2 new habits
- Keep going in less than a year you will be doing all of the ideas

> *"The only place success comes before work is in the dictionary"*
> —Vince Lombardi

What We Learned

Several years ago a young woman, named Jan, walked into the office to inquire about an open sales position. The position was to be the only sales person, selling for one of the smaller papers and work out of the office in that community. During the interview it was discovered that Jan had never sold print advertising before and had little sales experience. However, she did come across as a person that was focused and willing to learn. Jan said she did not mind putting in extra time to learn the job. Overall, she seemed like a good fit for the position and someone we could train.

It was decided that Jan would be hired and that we would train her at the paper's office instead of at the main office. That was done for 2 reasons. First of all, the sales manager would have to work with her on a regular basis. But most importantly, Jan would not be around the other sales people to pick up bad habits. For a long time, it was felt that the more seasoned sales people inadvertently taught the new sales person some poor selling skills or habits. This would be the perfect way to test that belief and train a new sales person.

The following are some of the things we learned about the selling skills taught by the other sales people.

1. We did not tell her that some people in her territory did not advertise. So she called on every business to introduce herself and discuss their advertising needs. She kept going back to these prospects and after awhile several started to run ads in the paper.
2. We did not tell Jan that spec ads would not work. We showed her how to make up simple spec ads and she went out and sold them.
3. We did not tell her that certain accounts were seasonal accounts. She called on them and got ads from many of them on a regular basis.
4. We did not tell her that certain accounts can be difficult. She made the calls and was willing to work with her accounts and with the challenging people.
5. We did not tell her that no one was in the store before 9 in the morning. She started calling on customers at 8 and found many of them already at work.
6. We did not tell Jan that decision makers go to lunch between 11:30 and 1:30 pm. She just kept on making sales calls and finding most of the decision makers in their place of business.
7. We did not tell her that no one buys ads on signature pages. She just called on people and sold the ads.
8. We did not tell Jan that setting goals was a waste of time. She set up goals for each month and did her best to surpass her goals. Every month Jan was selling more than in the previous month.

9. We did not tell her to put her regular customers in special sections. She sold special sections to customers that could benefit from being in the section.
10. We did not tell Jan that color was expensive and hard to sell. She just offered it to her customers and many of them bought it.
11. We did not tell her that people do not believe audit numbers. She was trained how to use the circulation audit during sales calls and she used the audit training to increase her sales.
12. We did not tell Jan that her hours were between 8 and 5. We told her she was full time. She soon found out that some customers, like building contractors need to be contacted early in the morning or late at night. That is what she did and created many new sales.
13. We did not tell her that joining civic organizations was a waste of time. She joined them, worked hard supporting them, networked, and became friends with many of her customers.
14. We did not tell Jan that selling advertising was done by going out to see customers and picking up ads. She just continued to take care of her customers and became a partner in the successful operation of their business.

Learning everything about an account or a territory from the other sales reps can be a real disservice to the new sales person and to the customers. Think back – do you have some selling skills or habits that need to be unlearned?

Action Steps:

- Go through the list above and select one bad habit you want to unlearn
- Develop a plan with a deadline to have the change implemented
- Do the same thing with another bad habit
- If you do anything for 30 days you have formed a new habit
- Continue to correct your bad habits

P.S. Jan is currently working as a national accounts manager for a large newspaper on the East coast.